Literacy, *Ideology,* and Dialogue

SUNY Series, Teacher Empowerment and School Reform
Henry A. Giroux and Peter L. McLaren, editors

Literacy, Ideology, and Dialogue

Towards a Dialogic Pedagogy

Irene Ward

STATE UNIVERSITY OF NEW YORK PRESS

Published by
State University of New York Press

©1994 State University of New York

All rights reserved

Printed in the United States of America

For information, address State University of New York Press, State
University Plaza, Albany, NY 12246

Production by Marilyn P. Semerad
Marketing by Bernadette LaManna

Library of Congress Cataloging–in–Publication Data

Ward, Irene, 1950–
    Literacy, ideology, and dialogue : towards a dialogic pedagogy /
Irene Ward.
            p.   cm. — (SUNY series, teacher empowerment and school
reform)
    Includes bibliographical references (p.   ) and index.
    ISBN 0-7914-2197-X (hard : acid–free paper). — ISBN 0-7914-2198-8
(paper : acid–free paper)
    1. Rhetoric—Study and teaching.   2. Communication in education.
I. Title. II. Series: Teacher empowerment and school reform.
P53.27.W37   1994
808´.007—dc20   94–4832
                                                                      CIP

10 9 8 7 6 5 4 3 2 1

For Merle and Bill

Contents

Acknowledgments

I wish to thank Gary A. Olson for providing the atmosphere in which I could undertake this project and for his dialogic engagement in the conception, writing, and editing of this book; Henry Giroux and David Bleich for their encouragement at crucial times, helping me believe; Joe Moxley, Sara Deats, Alma Bryant, and Richard Preto-Rodas for their careful reading, comments, and questions during the drafting process, as well as for their more than supportive friendship; Laura Sells for her warm friendship and for listening and talking at the oddest of hours and at very short notice; my colleagues at Kansas State University, especially Dean Hall, Dave Smit, Bonnie Nelson, and Tom Murray for their encouragement and excitement. Finally, Rebecca Albrecht, Kenda Morris, and Nina Marilyn Minor deserve recognition for their technical assistance, and the editorial staff at SUNY Press, especially Priscilla C. Ross, for her patience and encouragement in bringing the book to its present form.

Introduction

The larger context for this book about dialogue and composition theory and practice grows out of scholarly discussions of literacy education, discussions of the role that college-level composition courses have in furthering students' general literacy, discussions of various forms of student-centered and collaborative methodology, and the work of Jonathan Kozal and others in literacy theory. Dialogic teaching methods and the interactive nature of language learning have caught the attention of many educators and the discussion of the possible role of dialogue in teaching and learning is beginning to go on in other fields as well.[1]

College-level composition instructors have and will continue to have a rather interesting position in relation to all these developments. Many institutions of higher learning have been facing a number of pressures like open admissions, increasing numbers of nontraditional students, and public concern over a supposed or real literacy crisis in the United States. This group of instructors often have more freedom to experiment with their teaching, than their counterparts on the secondary level, and, for good or ill, often teach in circumstances that practically force them into devising pedagogy "on-the-spot" because traditional methods are often inadequate for their situation.

Many instructors at this level are employed by colleges and universities either as part of graduate programs or as instructors often without the requirement to spend significant amounts of time on research or service within the institution, and many of them teach as many as eight to ten sections of composition a year, creating situations where new knowledge about what works and how is gained by necessity rather than by design. Many of these same people become interested in teaching and its theories as an area scholarly inquiry while teaching postsecondary composition and later become professors. Andrea Lunsford, for instance, relates how she became interested in composition as a scholarly endeavor while teaching basic writing and needing help, which she generously received from Mina Shaughnessy ("Nature" 4). Composition studies has been a field that has grown from the bottom up. Many teaching assistants and instructors later go on to make contributions to what we know about writers, how they work, and how written discourse works in the world to get things done. The field has grown from the experience and problems that instructors have faced on Monday mornings. In some ways this book chronicles changes in composition theory and classroom methodology in the last twenty-five years and, I hope, adds to as well as points to emerging work that will have a major effect in this field.

Writing as a Dialogic Process

Many compositionists are abandoning the notion that written communication is a one-way process in which a reader decodes a message sent by a writer via the conduit of language. Replacing this view of written discourse is a much more complex one in which the writer, reader, and their cultural and historical contexts are implicated in the production of the text. Producing written discourse is a communicative, rhetorical, and, above all, dialogic process. The text, no longer seen as "authored" by a single individual, is conceived as being produced in a collaboration of individuals and institutions that both constrain and multiply its meaning, as a single strand in a vast web of linguistic, historical, and cultural factors. At present, a number of competing reading and writing theories attempt to account for all the factors that interact if discourse is to be understood, and compositionists are beginning to apply various dialogic theories of communication to the teaching of written discourse.

Proposals for using dialogic techniques in the composition classroom have been appearing in the scholarly literature with increasing frequency. There are three principal reasons for increased exploration of dialogism: the recognition by many educators of the importance of active student participation in the learning process, the need to provide effective education for students from diverse cultural and linguistic backgrounds, and the shift from structuralist to poststructuralist views of language and the ensuing implications for theories of reading and writing instruction. For many compositionists, dialogic pedagogies address the need for teaching methods that do not disadvantage some students simply because they are not linguistically or culturally part of the "mainstream." Given the U.S.'s promise of equal access to education, these pedagogies are seen by some as more just and empowering than traditional methods. Theorists with vastly differing theoretical assumptions such as Kenneth Bruffee and Ken Macrorie, Peter Elbow and Thomas Kent, and William Covino and Paulo Freire are all advocating dialogic classroom methodologies. Since composition scholars from radically different ideological and epistemological perspectives are advocating some form of dialogic pedagogy, it is reasonable to assume that the time has come for a reassessment of dialogic pedagogies for composition studies. This book examines current uses of dialogism in composition and proposes a functional and more comprehensive theory of dialogic pedagogy for composition.

Assumptions about Composition Instruction

I assume throughout this work that most student writing needs to be more than classroom practice. Students need to write for a variety of public as well as academic audiences. Writing courses should work toward increasing general public literacy, and not focus too narrowly on school literacy. What follows are several reasons why I believe this is so.

Susan Miller argues that the culmination of the history of writing instruction in the U.S. has resulted in a specific and distinct form of student literacy—a result of inhabiting a very specialized social and textual situation. Many compositionists have realized that there is a school discourse that is unlike discourse composed for other audiences and purposes (Ken Macrorie and James Britton are obvious early examples). As Miller explains, "Within the enclosed discourse of the school, student writing retains its status as practice—no matter how correct, 'original,' or provocative its text may be. It is always rehearsal, if dress rehearsal" (163). The classroom is a very difficult place to reproduce communicative interaction because of the artificiality of the rhetorical situation actually created. As Elbow has pointed out, "Teachers are one of the trickiest audiences of all" (*Writing With Power* 216). Instead of behaving like real audiences, teachers often become merely "skilled cataloguer[s] of weaknesses and (one hopes) strengths" (225). As a result, students experience "all the anxiety yet none of the satisfaction of practical writing" (228). In short, the way that composition is traditionally taught, even in the process paradigm, provides students with a rather limited form of literacy. Students who earn good grades by mastering academic forms and academic audience expectations may still be left without effective strategies for assessing the needs of other audiences. Therefore, writing assignments meant to allow students to demonstrate analysis and synthesis skills, for example, cannot be substituted for practice addressing a variety of audiences—that is, if we desire students to become fully literate.

Moreover, Miller and others contend that we cannot automatically expect that competence at one level of writing or in one rhetorical situation will transfer to others. She argues that each individual student's development as a writing subject in each new context is similar to Mina Shaughnessy's basic writers' struggles to enter the textual world of written discourse. For Miller, Shaughnessy's basic writer becomes "an active emblem for contemporary writing and for all of its writers' entries into unfamiliar textual worlds." That is, "Every writer is in some measure a basic writer" (165). Students of whatever proficiency who are entering new discourse communities are like the basic writer grappling with the rudiments of discourse production all over again.

The idea that learning to write may be a recursive rather than a hierarchical process has implications for assumptions about the transferability of writing skills. James Kinneavy, in an article that attempts to unravel the puzzle of how the levels of composition (grammar, usage, etc.) relate to the whole (the act of composing and the success of the final product), asks, "At what point(s) does transfer of grammatical, library, usage, and even logical skills take place so that they are effectively used in composition?" Kinneavy concludes that

> situational context seems to be the critical level. Only in the dialect [sic] with the situational context do the word, then the sentence, the section, and even the text encounter the real tentativeness, changing relationships, relativity, and reciprocal interdependence which are determinative. . . . In the classroom then, when we can pose real communication situations there is the highest likelihood

of transfer of skills. Otherwise the situational context has to be simulated. And the further away the level is from the situational context, the less likely is there to be the motivation to transfer. (312)

Michael Carter has come to a similar conclusion by applying the theory of expertise to composition: "There is no such thing as an expert writer in general. Writers become experts only within rhetorical contexts in which they gain much experience and facility" (65).

These theorists' ideas suggest that the more nearly composition pedagogy enacts the actual rhetorical situations of public discourse the more effective the pedagogy will be in producing students capable of composing effective discourse in a variety of situations. In short, I assume that the closer classrooms come to enacting, or actually do enact communication with others in order to get things done in the world the more effective the pedagogy will be. Composition courses should not solely be about the development of "academic discourse." Therefore, students should have ample opportunity to practice the kinds of discourse that attempts to get things done in their communities and, I audaciously hope, that will help them become interested, productive participants in democracy.

Literacy, Ideology, Dialogue

In chapter one I discuss the scholarship of expressivists Ken Macrorie, Donald Murray, and Peter Elbow. Although these compositionists employ dialogic methods in their classrooms, the overall goal of the pedagogy is each student's self–discovery. Newly discovered self–knowledge manifests itself by the emergence in the student's writing of an "authentic voice"—a

voice that is unique and that is able to reveal to others the
authentic perceptions, or "truth," of the student's experience
and by extension the universal truths of human experience.
Macrorie and Murray emphasize self-expression most heavily,
whereas Elbow recognizes a larger role for audiences and the
need for written discourse to communicate.

However, all three of these compositionists advocate placing
students in dialogue with each other in the writing classroom:
for Macrorie, students engage in dialogue in order to help one
another recognize the genuine and artificial in each other's
prose; for Murray, it's in order to help each other recognize
what composing strategies are most effective; for Elbow, it's in
order to act as "stand-ins" for future "real" audiences. Although each pedagogy advocates student dialogue, the dialogues are used to achieve slightly different goals in each case.
Moreover, each of these theorists sees writing as a one-way
process; the meaning of the discourse is coded by the writer and
decoded by readers. They do not perceive the writing event
itself as a transaction between people or an engagement in
dialogue. Much of this scholarship, with the possible exception
of Elbow's later work, is limited in that it attends almost
exclusively to students' processes of self-discovery through
writing, often at the expense of considerations of audience and
purpose.

In chapter two, I analyze the work of several compositionists
who consider writing as a social activity, one that involves
writers' interaction with language, readers, and culture. Social
constructionist theorists posit that knowledge is "made" in
interactions within and among knowledge communities.
Written discourse is viewed as a continuous dialogue in which
any particular written document is understood as an answer to
other already existing documents and is perceived to elicit a
response.

In this chapter, I discuss the work of Marilyn M. Cooper, Karen Burke LeFevre, Anne Ruggles Gere, and Kenneth A. Bruffee, all of whom attempt to provide theoretical links between social constructionism and composition theory. However, it is Bruffee who has been most influential and who has devised the most comprehensive pedagogical methods based on social constructionism. For example, his method of "peer criticism" is designed to mirror the interactions of discourse communities in society at large within the structure of the composition classroom. In the last section of this chapter, I discuss the ways that social constructionist composition methodology falls short of its promise as a more effective composition pedagogy.

Many of these theorists assume that dialogic pedagogies based in social constructionist theory necessarily lead to more democratic interaction and to student empowerment. I argue that the pedagogies described do not necessarily lead to the kind of classroom situations where truly democratic dialogue can take place. I conclude that it is naive to think that the power imbalances evident in social relationships outside the class-room—imbalances based on gender, race, ethnicity, and class, for instance—can be nullified inside the classroom simply by requiring students to work in groups and engage in dialogue.

In chapter three, I examine the scholarship of composition theorists who draw on the work of Brazilian literacy theorist Paulo Freire. Freire's pedagogy, developed largely in Third World countries, is based on a theory of dialogue and employs dialogic methodology that provides a radical alternative to traditional presentational pedagogy, what Freire calls the "bank-ing" model. Freire claims that traditional pedagogy dehuman-izes students by viewing them as objects that are acted upon by the instructor. Liberatory learning, in contrast, encourages students to take an active role in their education, becoming subjects (that is, agents) rather than objects. Both students and instructor actively engage in *praxis*—reflection plus action—a dialogic process that leads to personal and political consciousness, what Freire calls *conscientização*.

Freire's literacy theory has had rather disappointing results so far when North American compositionists have attempted to interpret it for postsecondary composition. I examine several scholarly accounts of these attempts, concluding that they fail in direct proportion to the degree to which they ignore or fail to apply the dialogic aspects of Freirean theory.

Chapter four examines recent attempts by compositionists to make connections between poststructuralist language theory and philosophy on the one hand, and composition theory and pedagogy on the other. Like liberatory learning theory, poststructuralist pedagogy also attempts to break down the traditional classroom hierarchy of master and pupil. This pedagogy is not based on an assumed universality and stability of truth and knowledge but, in contrast, understands that knowledge and truth unfold in interpretive, interactive, and communicative processes presumed to be much like the process of rhetorical invention. The goal of the pedagogy is not to (re)present stable knowledge for the student but for the student and instructor to "perform" the processes to be learned.

This chapter draws on Gregory Ulmer's conception of poststructuralist pedagogy as an explicit linking of rhetorical invention and performance to provide a concept of poststructuralist pedagogy in general. Then I analyze the work of William A. Covino, who presents a revisionist reading of classical rhetorical history from a poststructuralist perspective in order to recover aspects of classical rhetoric that recognize the value of ambiguity, multiple perspectives, and openendedness. In light of his reinterpretation, Covino suggests that composition courses focus on genres uncommon to the expository writing classroom, such as dialogue and drama. This pedagogy would shift the emphasis of the writing curriculum away from more traditional academic forms that demand closure and certainty. He proposes a dialogic pedagogy that would allow students to explore multiple perspectives without necessarily declaring any final conclusions, thus always inviting the dialogue to continue.

Unfortunately, although Covino asks students to use discourse forms that enact dialogic situations, the situation in which the students themselves write remains monologic rather than dialogic. The interaction in the classroom remains primarily between the instructor and each individual student; collaborative situations are offered only as options and are in no way integral to the pedagogy. Moreover, each student's written discourse is directed to the instructor for the purpose of being graded, never to any other audience capable of providing a response. Hence the student's writing remains an arhetorical "writing exercise" because it does not perform a communicative interaction.

In the last section of chapter four, I examine the extensive scholarship of Thomas Kent. Drawing on works by Jacques Derrida, Donald Davidson, and others, Kent criticizes several basic assumptions of social constructionist theory and provides a tentative, yet convincing, theoretical underpinning for a poststructuralist dialogic pedagogy. Kent claims that writing and reading are fundamentally activities that involve the reader and writer in "hermeneutic guessing"—a dialogic process of making interpretive guesses about what other people will understand. These guessing strategies are not systematizable, since no two dialogic situations are ever *exactly* the same. Therefore, Kent argues, the goal of discourse education is to provide situations in which students have the opportunity to refine their hermeneutic guessing strategies. These strategies can only be refined in *dialogic* situations in which students engage in communicative interaction and, thereby, gain immediate feedback regarding the degree of success of their guess. In other words, communicative interaction is what is performed in the classroom. Unfortunately, Kent's work, as yet, draws too heavily on speaking situations to exemplify his ideas and, perhaps, goes too far in dismissing the concept of discourse community and in negating the importance of convention in the understanding of discourse. I end by drawing some conclusions about the nature and potential of poststructuralist composition theory.

Chapter five synthesizes concepts of dialogue discussed in the previous four chapters and attempts to posit a more functional and comprehensive theory of dialogic pedagogy. A comprehensive dialogic pedagogy would recognize that knowledge unfolds in the process of attempting to communicate with others; in the give–and–take of this process, people come to know themselves, other people, and something about the concrete world. Another important component would be the development of students' ability to engage in dialogue with internalized others—what is traditionally called reflective thought. However, the goal of internal dialogue is "ideological becoming," a relational rather than personal concept of knowing—that is, the recognition of how one's personal knowledge is related to the knowledge of various communities and the unequal power structures that affect that interaction. In addition, as students encounter the voices of others in written documents, the voices of other writers help shape their internally persuasive discourse.

Peer criticism, another component of dialogic pedagogy, is one of the most productive ways that students in a writing class engage in communicative interaction because they are dealing with concrete audiences whose responses are timely enough to be considered, incorporated or not, responded to or not. A productive dialogic pedagogy would also encourage students to address written documents to public audiences with the purpose of having some effect on those they address, because, as I argue earlier, the closer composition pedagogy comes to performing actual rhetorical situations of public discourse the more effective the pedagogy is likely to be.

What has been missing in composition's concepts of dialogic pedagogy is an acknowledgment of differences among students and how the unequal social structures of society at large—structures related to racism, sexism, and classism—affect classroom settings in ways that disadvantage some and privilege others. I address this issue by using philosopher Lorraine Code's revision of traditional epistemology and Sharon Welch's concept of communicative ethics as ways to help instructors and students become conscious of the ways democratic dialogue can be curtailed by uneven access to dialogic interaction and to assist them in discovering ways that avoid reproducing the negative effects of sexism, racism, and classism in composition classrooms by openly incorporating an ethical stance to equal participation on the part of all students. Most importantly, a comprehensive dialogic pedagogy is one of inclusion; it is a pedagogy that acts to encourage all students to attempt to find a place in higher education regardless of their particular "differences."

As dialogism becomes more and more central to composition theory and pedagogy, it is essential that compositionists strive to break out of narrow ideological orientations and to embrace a more comprehensive notion of dialogism. The synthetic, functional dialogism that I have sketched here is but a beginning. What is needed now is more full–scale investigations into the social and psychological dynamics of dialogic interaction. Such investigations could eventually contribute to an even fuller and more useful dialogism that is appropriate for the composition classroom. What *is* certain, though, is that dialogism has become fundamental to modern composition pedagogy. Only through dialogue will students learn to be able to adopt a subject position in the conversation of humankind. This book attempts to provide much-needed perspective on the theories and uses of dialogic pedagogy in composition studies and the classrooms where such ideas are enacted.

Note

1. See for instance, Ronald C. Arnett, Deborah Brandt, and Henry Giroux.

Expressivists: Self-Discovery and Internal Dialogue

> The purpose... is to help you achieve, through writing, a new level of self-discovery. And the best evidence of this self-discovery will be the emergence in your writing of an authentic voice.
>
> —Stewart, *The Authentic Voice*

This chapter discusses the dialogic pedagogies of three composition theorists classed together, rather uneasily, as expressivists (sometimes called expressionists).[1] These three theorists—Ken Macrorie, Peter Elbow, and Donald Murray—have devised pedagogies that are explicitly dialogic. William Coles, Jr., and Donald Stewart, the other theorists most often mentioned as expressivists, do not employ or advocate dialogic teaching methods to a significant degree.[2]

Although Donald Stewart's pedagogy is not dialogic, the epigraph above states rather clearly a basic assumption of expressivist rhetoric: that the student comes to know himself or herself through language. As James Berlin writes:

This type of expressionistic rhetoric focuses on a dialectic between the individual and language as a means of getting in touch with the self. Indeed, even the dialectic between the writer and the editorial group is designed to enable the writer to understand the manifestation of her identity in language through considering the reactions of others. (*Rhetoric and Reality* 153)

Another common assumption is that writing cannot be taught, though it can be learned. For example, Elbow writes:

In proposing the teacherless writing class I am trying to deny something—something that is often assumed: *the necessary connection between learning and teaching.* The teacherless writing class is a place where there is learning but no teaching. (*Writing Without Teachers* ix)

This assumption is common to many of the theorists who have devised or advocate dialogic pedagogies (as will be demonstrated in later chapters). According to these compositionists, the role of the instructor is to provide an environment where the student can gain experience with writing, acting not as instructor so much as experienced coach or master craftsperson whom one consults as needed. In these classroom situations, students engage in dialogue with each other and with the instructor in order to provide one another with feedback about their writing processes and the work in progress. Each theorist's concept of the nature of the dialogue is different, leading to differing goals and outcomes for the students, though the theoretical assumptions underlying the work of all the expressivists unifies them and their work.

Dialogic "Helping Circles" and the Search for Truth

One day late in 1963, a student stopped Ken Macrorie in the hall and asked him to respond to a comment she had written about another teacher. The now famous passage reads like this:

He finks it humorous to act like the Grape God Almighty,
only the stridents in his glass lisdyke him immersely. Day
each that we tumble into the glass he sez to mee. "Eets too
badly that you someday fright preach Engfish." (*Uptaught*
18)

From this passage (a parody of James Joyce's prose), Macrorie
borrowed the term "Engfish" to name the kind of dead prose
that he deplored and found everywhere. He describes this kind
of prose as "bloated, pretentious language" and a "feel–nothing,
say–nothing language, dead like Latin, devoid of the rhythms
of contemporary speech" (*Uptaught* 18). He blames traditional
teaching methods as the cause of "say–nothing" student papers:

> Traditionally, unwittingly, over the centuries school has
> become a place where you and I were handed things—
> usually statements or combinations of numbers belonging
> to school or "the authorities." We were to hand them
> back to teacher in the form of answers to tests or papers
> (collages of excerpted statements by authorities or
> summaries of what they had said). . . . This handing back
> and forth of ideas and experience belonging to school left
> no room for students' experience, which must enter the
> transaction somewhere or there can be no relevance to
> learning.[3] (*Telling Writing* 289)

To counteract such ineffective teaching methods, at least in
his own specialty, Macrorie searched for more effective ways
to teach writing; his quest was to devise ways to teach students
to produce lively prose rather than the Engfish found everywhere in schools. He derived two major pedagogical tools
from his experimentation: "writing freely" and the "helping
circle."

The now universally familiar technique of freewriting arose from Macrorie's frustration. By 1964, he had become so exasperated with the stilted Engfish of student papers that he told his students to "go home and write anything that comes to your mind. Don't stop. Write for ten minutes or till you've filled a whole page" (*Uptaught* 20). He began experimenting with the method he called "writing freely."[4] Gradually, the students' papers began to improve and flashes of life started to appear in their prose. He believed he had found a teaching method that helped students bypass Engfish and find their authentic voices.

In the "helping circle," students read each other's writing and help one another recognize when they have found their authentic voice. Macrorie reproduces a student's writing for the group members; then a student reads it aloud and the classmates respond. The students, having been exposed to numerous examples of Engfish early in the term, can eventually distinguish living from dead prose. The antidote Macrorie advocates for Engfish is "truthtelling." Through writing freely and the honest response of their peers, students break through their proclivity for Engfish and can discover their authentic voice—the source of truthtelling. The authentic voice objectifies the writer's experience, allowing a reader to "live it vicariously and a writer [to] re-experience it" (*Telling Writing* 286).

In *Telling Writing*, Macrorie's college–level composition textbook, he provides sample student papers and a narrative with dialogue from a fictional helping circle rather than describing what the dialogue should be like. He remains general about the nature of the dialogue and what should happen in the circle, providing six guidelines:

1. Avoid beginning comments about a writing with small points. First, let the writer know your large

reaction, especially if it's positive. Then later in the discussion bring up the small suggestion; for example, to cut a word or change a phrase.

2. If you're the leader in the circle, don't let an argument drag on about a point that has been discussed fully. You can say, "Well, John has now been given several alternatives. He can take them home and decide which one he wants to use in rewriting his work, or he can turn down all of them." The circle is not a debating society but a gathering of helpers.

3. If you find yourself talking too much or too little, remember that the most helpful responder presents his best thought—the one most apt to surprise and be useful. He resists the impulse to make obvious comments.

4. If you feel reluctant to talk. think [sic] of your responsibility to others. Responsibility—ability to respond. There's no other you in the world. No other person with the same set of past experiences. Only you can say what you feel and think, what *your* response to a writing was. That's what every serious writer is looking for: the effect of his writing upon individuals. You can't say anything wrong to him if you truthfully report your response to his work. And you may help him a lot.

5. Occasionally close your eyes while listening to a writing being read. But only in a circle whose members already know that listeners are apt to do that on purpose, not because they're bored.

6. As a responder you can sometimes draw out another responder who's reluctant to speak fully his feelings.

"You said the story was too cute. Can you say more
about why you felt that way?" (87)

Early in the course, Macrorie disallows any negative comments, believing that students need to build on successes before
they can handle what may be poorly done in what they have
written. Writes Macrorie, "After they've received praise from
the group, writers are usually strong enough to listen to others
tell them that a subsequent work is weak in large ways.
Eventually every writer must learn to use negative comments
to improve her work" (285). Also, he refrains from responding
to students' writing until the helping circle has done so, fearing
that rather than provide their own responses the students
would imitate him in an effort to please him. The helping
circle, according to Macrorie, is the "third best resource" for
feedback a writer can use to improve his or her writing:

The circle—at times frightening to every writer—is her
third best resource. First, her own experience (including
thoughts, feelings, and knowledge she picks up from
others). Second, her skills as a writer. And third, the help
the circle gives her to sharpen and hone those skills. (74)

The helping circle's purpose is to increase writers' ability to
judge their own writing. The object of the students' dialogue
in the helping circle is to assist each other in recognizing when
they are "truthtelling"—when what they have written is believ-
able as a reflection of their "authentic" experience.

Another dialogic aspect of Macrorie's work is his recommendation that student writing be "published" in some way—
even mimeographed copies posted on bulletin boards would
do. The promise of publication shifts some of the students'
focus away from the instructor as audience and takes the

students' writing to the realm beyond the classroom. The student has the experience of dialogue, knowing that his or her writing will be read by a wider audience than the instructor; and this promise, Macrorie claims, motivates students to revise and polish their work.

In short, the goal of Macrorie's dialogic pedagogy is to eliminate Engfish from students' writing. The dialogic group acts to reinforce students' efforts at "truthtelling." The expected outcome is clearer, more lively prose that actually reflects the true, honest experience of the writer.

Macrorie accomplishes these goals by employing freewriting techniques, helping circles, and opportunities for students to "publish" their papers. Other expressivists, especially Donald Murray, share Macrorie's desire to promote "authentic self-expression" and employ dialogic group activities to effect this objective. In fact, Murray has gained the reputation among many scholars as the model expressivist because of his thoroughly neo-romantic view of the writing process.

Writing as a Discovery of Self

Donald Murray argues that writers write to understand, not be understood: "For the writer, writing is a process, a way of seeing, of hearing what he has to say to himself, a means of discovering meaning" ("Explorers" 4). According to Murray, writers are not as concerned with communication as they are with exploring their own identity and discovering who they are. For example, here are representative statements from three of Murray's better known essays:

When we discover what we have said we discover who we are. In finding your voice you discover your identity. Style is not a fashionable garment you put on; style is what you are; what you have to say as well as how you say it.

. . . We write to explore the constellations and galaxies which lie unseen within us waiting to be mapped with our own words. . . . The writer goes on writing to discover, explore, and map the evolution of personal world of inner space. ("Explorers" 7)

To communicate effectively the writer may do some final tinkering and make some adjustments in his words, using specialized analogies, for example, to reach a particular audience. But even in the final editing the professional writer doesn't look to the language, but through it to what he has to say. . . . The writer doesn't make adjustments in what he has to say; he doesn't look to the audience first and write down what the reader wants to hear. The good writer communicates by building—through language—a sturdy discovery of thought. ("Interior View" 11)

We are motivated to write when we communicate to ourselves. Others come later or not at all. It is satisfying to share, to entertain, to explain, to persuade, to reach an audience, but it is a great, private joy to hear yourself, to be quiet and to listen to the music of your own meaning wrestling itself free of confusion, to see a page on which your hint of potential meaning stands free of you, rooted in its own understanding. ("What Makes" 111)

Clearly, Murray emphasizes the writer's communication with himself or herself—the writer's personal discovery of his or her identity—over communication with others. The motivating drive to write is not the desire to engage in dialogue with others but to know one's self. Communication—dialogue with others—is almost a by-product of the activity of writing. Nevertheless, Murray is a champion of dialogic pedagogy.

Rather than dialogue with others to advance communication, however, Murray promotes dialogue with the self.

Dialogue with the Other Self

Murray's dialogic pedagogy aims to develop the writer's "other self." The other self, he claims, is the "writer's first reader." In Murray's concept, the other self becomes the monitor for the entire writing process. He likens the other self to an explorer or a mapmaker:

> The other self scans the entire territory, forgetting, for the moment, questions of order or language. The writer/ explorer looks for the draft's horizons. Once the writer has scanned the larger vision of the territory, it may be possible to trace a trail that will get the writer from here to there, from meaning identified to meaning clarified. Questions of order are now addressed, but questions of language still delayed. Finally, the writer/explorer studies the map in detail to spot the hazards that lie along the trail, the hidden swamps of syntax, the underbrush of verbiage, the voice found, lost, found again. ("Teaching the Other Self" 166)

This other self not only knows what is actually on the page but also understands the writer's process so far, projects into the future what possible shapes the work might yet take, and, more importantly, follows "thinking that has not yet become thought" (166). It monitors the thinking processes, pursuing "a wisp of thinking until it grows into a completed thought" (165). The other self, in dialogue with the self, performs many functions—many that involve higher order thinking skills.

Murray complains that composition research has not fully documented the role of the other self in the writing process, but he cites the work of researchers like Sondra Perl and Nancy Sommers as a beginning of this investigation. He predicts that such research will reveal several functions that the other self performs during the writing process:

- The other self tracks the activity that is taking place. Writing, in a sense, does not exist until it is read. The other self records the evolving text.

- The other self gives the self the distance that is essential for craft. This distance, the craftperson's step backwards, is a key element in that writing that is therapeutic for the writer.

- The other self provides an evolving context for the writer. As the writer adds, cuts, or records, the other self keeps track of how each change affects the draft.

- The other self articulates the process of writing, providing that writer with an engineering history of the developing text, a technical resource that records the problems faced and the solutions that were tried and rejected, not yet tried, and the one that is in place.

- The other self is the critic who is continually looking at the writing to see if, in the writer's phrase, "it works."

- The other self also is the supportive colleague to the writer, the chap who commiserates and encourages, listens sympathetically to the writer's complaints and reminds the writer of past success. The deeper we get into the writing process the more we may discover how affective concerns govern the cognitive, for writing is an intellectual activity carried on in an emotional environment, a precisely engineered sailboat trying to hold course in a vast and stormy

Atlantic. The captain has to deal with fears as well as compass readings. (166–67)

It is this other self that inexperienced writers (and writing instructors) are not cognizant of and that Murray's method claims to "make articulate."

Murray's Dialogic Conference Method

Murray claims that frequent, brief, individual conferences are the best technique for helping students develop the other self. In these conferences the instructor must let the student speak first about work in progress; then the instructor responds to the student's response. The instructor can ask such open–ended questions as, "What surprised you? What's working best? What are you going to do next?" However, the instructor cannot give directions or respond to the writing directly, as in Macrorie's or Elbow's model of dialogic pedagogy. Instead, the instructor must respond only to what the student says about the writing process at that particular stage. Murray is not an audience for the writing, as in Macrorie or Elbow (see below); he is a coach for the other self. He gives this example:

With remedial students I am handed a text that I simply cannot understand. I do not know what it is supposed to say. I can not discover a pattern of organization. I can not understand the language. But when the writer tells me what the writer was doing, when the other self is allowed to speak, I find that the text was produced rationally. The writer followed misunderstood instruction, inappropriate principles, or logical processes that did not work. (168)

Rather than informing the student what is wrong with the draft, Murray responds to the student's response to his or her own writing process.

In the short dialogue of the conference, Murray can confirm or correct students' writing or thinking processes. He found that "writers' feelings control the environment in which the mind functions" and noticed that male writers often express a false confidence and women writers a false modesty. In these situations, he must deal with these "false" feelings by supporting "the other self that knows how good the work really is" (169).

One reason that he does not deal directly and primarily with the text the student presents to him in the conference is that he finds that similar looking drafts can be accompanied by different perceptions held by the writer:

> I am constantly astonished when I see drafts of equal accomplishment but with writer evaluations that are miles apart. One student may say, "This is terrible. I can't write. I think I'd better drop the course." And right after that on a similar paper a student says, "I never had so much fun writing before. I think this is a really good paper. Do you think I should become a writer?" (169)

In each case, without knowing how the writer evaluates his or her writing, the instructor runs the risk of continuing the student's faulty self-evaluations and preventing the student from being able to take the appropriate action to improve the draft. The goal of the conference is to allow writers to produce increasingly better drafts, to keep revising until the meaning becomes clear both to the student and the instructor.

This dialogic one-on-one conferencing is reinforced in the classroom in small- and large-group workshops:

The same dynamics take place as have been modeled in the conference. The group leader asks the writer, "How can we help you?" The other self speaks of the process or of the text. The workshop members listen and read the text with the words of the other self in their ears. Then they respond, helping the other self become a more effective reader of the evolving text. (171)

The conference and workshop experiences allow students to focus on what is working well, not on failure and error. Murray claims that successful writers don't "so much correct error as discover what is working and extend that element in the writing" (170). Murray's dialogic conferencing method allows students to focus on and build upon success.

As the semester moves along, Murray no longer needs to ask the opening question; the students come in and tell him where they are in a draft and what they plan to do next. When this happens, he finds that the best learning takes place if he merely makes explicit for the students what they have learned from the process so far, making the other self aware of the successful processes and reinforcing them so that they can become part of the writer's general repertoire of strategies.

The goal of the dialogue in Murray's pedagogy is to provide responses so that students can come to know themselves through an interaction with language and to express what they have found to be "true" through this personal inquiry. The response provided to writers and to their "other selves" assists their look inward. However, Murray does not conceive of the other self solely as an internal audience concept. The other self is also a specific kind of internal, mental manager who, if trained well, keeps the writing process moving. This concept of "internal audience" is not unique to Murray; it is also central to the work of Peter Elbow.

Dialogue and the Teacherless Class

Peter Elbow never uses the terms *dialogic* or *dialogism* to describe his pedagogy; however, his pedagogy is thoroughly dialogic in that much of the classroom activity he describes involves students talking to each other about their writing. Students converse about what each student has written in order to provide immediate feedback to each writer about his or her composition. Two key concepts of Elbow's pedagogy are dialogic: his notion of the "teacherless classroom" and his discussion of how concepts of audience can hinder and enhance one's composing process.

In *Writing Without Teachers*, Elbow argues that the best way to learn to write more effectively is with a "teacherless writing class." This class can be formed by a group of individuals whether or not they are formally enrolled in a writing class. Also, writing teachers can base their classes on this model as well. (If they do, they must also agree to write and share something every week as full, equal participants.) Like the liberatory learning model discussed in chapter three, the teacher's role in Elbow's pedagogy is not that of expert but is closer to the role of fellow student/writer.

Elbow argues that it is difficult, especially for inexperienced writers, to compose without direct and immediate feedback from a variety of readers. Feedback is important to any writer's development: a writer has to know what effects his or her words are having on readers. As Elbow writes, "You need movies of people's minds while they read your words" (*Writing Without Teachers* 77). Thus, the dialogue in the classroom is designed to give the writer a representation of what has gone on in the minds of readers when they have read his or her words. In contrast to Macrorie and Murray, Elbow is more aware of the communicative function of written discourse and is interested in helping writers experience how their writing affects others, including fellow students and the "real" audience that the writing may be intended for.

Thus, the dialogue in Elbow's pedagogy is among the students and is about their writing. The purpose of the teacherless class is to provide dialogic feedback to writers in advance of a real audience. The dialogue is not explicitly perceived to be between the "real" audience and the writer, as it is in social epistemic theory (discussed in chapter two), but between writers trying to help each other discover through dialogue what to say and the most effective way to say it. The ultimate objective of this pedagogy is for writers to gain enough experience so that they no longer need the group but can depend on their own sense of what is appropriate—that is, to be able to cope successfully with one's writing processes *independent* of others.

According to Elbow, the teacherless class should be formed from a small but diverse group of dedicated writers, and the group must commit to write something every week and to respond to everyone else's work faithfully. Elbow acknowledges that at first members may come and go until rapport develops among the members. Ideally, the group should have seven to twelve regular members who attend every week for a minimum of ten weeks.

Each group member brings to each session something he or she has written, anything from a business letter or report to a poem. The member reads the document aloud twice, and then the other members tell the writer how the writing has affected them (this response can be oral or written). In contrast to Macrorie's pedagogy, the kind of feedback envisioned in *Writing Without Teachers* is *nonevaluative*, one in which readers simply verbalize their reactions *as readers*. The goal is not to judge the writing good or bad or to suggest ways to improve it, although that may happen along the way; the object is simply to describe one's reactions to the words on the page so that the writer gains an accurate sense of how his or her prose is being received by readers.

After a writer reads the text, he or she listens while the other group members speak or write about the text. According to Elbow's scheme, the writers must not reveal how they feel about the reactions to their writing. If the readers sense that there is defensiveness on the writer's part, they will censor what they say and the writer will not obtain an accurate picture of readers' experiences. The writer must listen and absorb what is said. As Elbow advises writers, "Just take it all in. Assume that when you write something else—or rewrite this piece—your *own* choices about how to write it will organically benefit from hearing what they are now saying" (105).

Elbow has devised several classroom techniques to make this dialogic feedback more efficient and consistent for the reader. For example, he proposes four strategies for getting the dialogue underway: pointing, summarizing, telling, and showing. In *pointing*, the reader underlines words or passages that seem particularly effective:

> Start by simply pointing to the words and phrases which most successfully penetrated your skull: perhaps they seemed loud or full of voice; or they seemed to have a lot of energy; or they somehow rang true; or they carried special conviction. (85)

Elbow recommends a wavy line for any passages that the reader finds "particularly weak or empty" (86). These underlinings not only mark the strong and weak points of the text for the writer, but they also work as mnemonic devices for the "telling" stage when the reader explains what kind of "getting through" actually happened. If a composition is read aloud, pointing consists of recalling words and phrases and jotting them down after the reading ends.

The second stage, *summarizing*, contains four steps:

a) First tell very quickly what you found to be the main points, main feelings, or centers of gravity. Just sort of say what comes to mind for fifteen seconds, for example., "Let's see, very sad; the death seemed to be the main event; um . . . but the joke she told was very prominent; lots of clothes."

b) Then summarize it into a single sentence.

c) Then choose *one word* from the writing which best summarizes it.

d) Then choose a word that isn't in the writing to summarize it. (86)

Elbow considers pointing and summarizing the most efficient and accurate ways readers use to communicate perceptions to a writer during the dialogue that follows; the other methods can be skipped if time is short, but a class should always point and summarize (87).

In *telling*, the reader provides a narrative of what happened while he or she read: "And I felt this. . . . Then this happened," and so on. The listeners simply provide a short narrative about their reactions, not about how good or bad the writing was perceived to be. According to Elbow, some responses to writing cannot be communicated directly. *Showing* is a process of selecting an appropriate metaphor that "tap[s] knowledge which you have but which is usually unavailable to you" (90). Elbow provides a list of twenty-four possible ways to unearth descriptive metaphors of your reaction to a particular piece of writing. Here are five examples:

a. Talk about the writing as though you were describing *voices*: for example, shouting, whining, whispering, lecturing sternly, droning, speaking abstractly, and so forth. Try to apply such words not only to the whole thing but to different parts.

b. Talk about the writing as though you were talking about *motion* or *locomotion*: for example, as marching, climbing, crawling, rolling along, tiptoeing, strolling, sprinting, and so forth.

c. *Color:* What color is the whole? the parts?

d. The writing is a lump of workable clay. Tell what you would do with that clay.

e. Let your whole body make the movements inspired by the writing or different parts of it. Perhaps combine sounds and movements. (90–92)

Elbow claims that successful use of showing is often a function of the individual classes: some classes have simply been too shy to use them; others found them helpful and enjoyable.

These four classroom activities are ways that students engage in focused dialogue with each other in order to provide information about how a piece of writing has affected them. As Elbow says in several places, these are ways of letting writers know what is actually "getting into" the reader's head.

Dialogic response or feedback, according to Elbow, enhances one's development as a writer, especially in the early stages when the writer has little experience with how his or her written words affect others. It is difficult to obtain feedback about one's writing because of the special attention it takes from a reader and because much of the reaction is hidden from the writer unless the reader can verbalize reactions in dialogue with the author on the spot.

Criterion-Based and Reader-Based Feedback

In *Writing With Power*, Elbow refines the concept of feedback described in *Writing Without Teachers*, calling it reader-based feedback, and he adds a new category: criterion-based feedback. The two types of feedback provide the writer with different kinds of information. Criterion-based feedback assists a writer in discovering whether the piece of writing meets the criteria "most often used in judging expository or nonfiction writing." Reader-based feedback, like the concept of feedback discussed earlier, "tells you what your writing does to particular readers" (240). In practice the two kinds of criteria are not so easily distinguished from one another. As Elbow writes, "A reader cannot possibly give you a piece of criterion-based feedback except from the basis of something having happened inside him; nor can a reader give you a piece of reader-based feedback without at least implying a criterion of judgment or perception" (241).

Elbow offers lists of questions, heuristics, that writers can use to initiate dialogue with anyone about writing, no longer limiting the dialogic situation to a teacherless classroom. For criterion-based feedback, the questions range over these four areas:

a. What is the quality of the content of the writing: the ideas, the perceptions, the point of view?

b. How well is the writing organized?

c. How effective is the language?

d. Are there mistakes or inappropriate choices in usage?

For reader-based feedback, Elbow offers these questions:

a. What was happening to you, moment by moment, as you were reading the piece of writing?

b. Summarize the writing: give your understanding of what it says or what happened in it.

c. Make up some images for the writing and the transaction it creates with you. (240)

These heuristics become scripts for starting and directing dialogues with friends, teachers, or anyone who reads one's writing.

The writer, according to Elbow, should remain in control of the kind and, it is hoped, the quality of the feedback received from readers. Simply presenting writing to someone and asking what he or she thinks leaves the reader open to say anything or nothing. A writer's friends and family are often unwilling to criticize for fear of hurt feelings. People with little experience responding to writing may not readily be able to provide a reader with the kind of responses needed during the writing process. However, once a writer approaches a potential reader with specific questions, the resulting dialogue can be much more productive.

Elbow summarizes the benefits of each kind of feedback as follows:

> In short, the two kinds of feedback encourage readers to take different roles. When you ask a reader to give you criterion–based feedback you encourage him to function like an expert, a coach, or a commentator, that is, to stand off to the side and watch you from the stage wings as you give your violin concert and not to get too involved in your music. This helps him to tell you about your technique. When you ask your reader to give you reader–based feedback, on the other hand, you encourage him to

function like an audience, that is, to sit right out there in front of you and experience your music. This helps him tell you what your music does to the audience. (251)

Each dialogic role a writer asks readers to play provides a different slant on the response the writer is likely to receive from the "real" audience for the writing.

Sharing and Responding to Writing

Although *Writing Without Teachers* and *Writing With Power* were often used as classroom textbooks, they were primarily designed as trade publications directed at a general audience of people who experienced trouble with their writing. In 1989, Elbow and Pat Belanoff published a mainstream first-year college composition textbook, *A Community of Writers: A Workshop Course in Writing*, that represents a further refinement of Elbow's concepts of dialogic feedback. *A Community of Writers* comes packaged from the publisher with a separate, brief booklet titled *Sharing and Responding* that sets out a detailed list of questions designed to allow students to initiate productive dialogues about their writing. Elbow and Belanoff now claim that the kinds of feedback need to be sequenced:

> We have found that it is crucial to start with sharing and then move on to nonjudgmental kinds of responding before opening up to full criticism. This means moving from safety to risk. The progression builds trust: trust in yourself and in the others you work with. You can't give good responses to writing or benefit from them except in a situation of trust.[5] (1)

In short, Elbow asks students to engage in dialogue among themselves about their writing in progress in order to provide each other with specific kinds of response: descriptions of how the writing affected them or, later, how the writing may measure up to standards of "good writing." The writer is to use or discard this information—or just absorb the response.

In contrast to Macrorie's and Murray's emphasis on the authentic and honest self-expression, in Elbow's dialogic pedagogy the students "stand in" for the "real" audience, giving the writer a chance to experience how a real audience might respond. Although writers are often cautioned to use the writing process, and especially freewriting, to find out what they have to say *for themselves*, the dialogic groups are intended as a way to try one's writing out before it is made public or addressed to its intended audience.

The next section addresses Elbow's concepts of audience and how they can also be seen in dialogic terms and what pedagogical value they may have when conceived in these terms.

Elbow's Internal Dialogues

Elbow writes at length in *Writing With Power* and in "Closing My Eyes As I Speak: An Argument for Ignoring Audience" about how concepts of audience and different relationships with audiences can either hinder or enable the writer. He makes a series of distinctions about audience relationships, drawing attention to them so that writers can learn how to manipulate audience concepts in order to avoid losing focus or becoming blocked. These various ways of manipulating one's concepts of audience are ways of carrying on a series of internal dialogues with the self that, in the best of situations, enable a writer to explore and refine ideas.

I would argue, I think with Elbow's assent, that enabling concepts of audience become enabling metaphors for different types of internal dialogue. In many ways, these internal dialogues with various internal audiences become part of an extended invention process. The task is to gain control over and consistently employ those enabling audiences to help writers "find more to say and find better ways to say it" (*Writing With Power* 179).

Elbow himself resists seeing what he calls "private writing" as entirely an internal yet nevertheless "social" dialogue with the self. I believe, however, that the process of using these various enabling audience concepts activates the different kinds of internal dialogic processes necessary for producing effective written discourse. Below I discuss Elbow's concepts of audience and his suggestions about how to manipulate such concepts, and I address the internal social and therefore *dialogic* nature of his understanding of audience and how this conception is an unacknowledged part of Elbow's dialogic pedagogy, even despite his own resistance.

Elbow's Paradoxical Audience

Paradox is the organizing theme of Elbow's chapters on audience in *Writing With Power*. He sees three paradoxes that inform his exploration of the complex subject of audience in writing situations:

- Writing is usually a communication with others. And yet the essential transaction seems to be with oneself, a speaking to one's best self.

- Sometimes you can't figure out what you want to say and how to say it till you get into the presence of your audience (or think intensely about it). Yet sometimes it's only by getting *away* from your audience that you can figure out your meaning and how to convey it clearly: your real audience can distract or inhibit you.

- You can't get an audience to listen and hear you till you have something to say and can say it well. Yet I think the process by which people actually learn to speak and write well is often the other way around: first they get an audience that listens and hears them (parents first, then supportive teachers, then a circle of friends or fellow writers, and finally a larger audience). Having an audience helps them find more to say and find better ways to say it. (179)

According to Elbow, "dangerous" and "safe" audiences are partly an objective matter: either they are hostile critics, or they are supportive friends. On the other hand, these notions of audience are also subjective: "Some people are terrified no matter how friendly the audience is, while others are not intimidated even by sharks" (184–85). Here is what Elbow says about dangerous and safe audiences:

Dangerous Audience. When you experience an audience as dangerous: (a) it may make you so anxious that you actually cannot write at all; or (b) it may make you merely nervous, preoccupied with mistakes you might make, unable to find words naturally and smoothly, and, hence, unable to concentrate easily on your thoughts; or (c) it may not inhibit words or thoughts at all, but lead you into a protective voice which makes you feel safer, but drains your language of power.
Safe Audience. When, on the other hand, you experience an audience as safe or eliciting, it opens you out: you think of more ideas, feelings and images; words come more easily. But on a few occasions a safe audience can threaten you by making you feel things inside you that you'd rather not feel. (187–88)

In addition, Elbow also distinguishes between the "real audience," those people who will actually read the writing, and the audience that "we carry around inside our heads" or with whom we carry on an internal dialogue (186). Often the audience in our heads, the "habitual way of relating to readers-in-general," is dangerous and can distort perceptions of the real audience, causing false or inappropriate reactions in certain rhetorical situations (186). According to Elbow, the interaction of these four audience concepts—safe and dangerous, real and "in-our-head" audiences—affect both the quality and quantity of writing.

One of the secrets to "writing with power" is to find the audience concept that enables you, according to Elbow—even if, at first, it has little relation to the "real" audience. The enabling audience may be different at different stages in the writing process and for different situations. For example, in the early stages, thinking too much about the real audience, especially if it is also a dangerous one, can hinder a writer's progress. Later on, "wallowing in safety" can make the writing dull and lacking in excitement. The writer may need to envision a dangerous audience in order to sharpen the focus or liven things up. Sometimes expressing anger at a dangerous audience can produce clear, strong statements (*Writing With Power* 188–90, passim).

Internal Dialogics: Manipulating Audience Concepts

I see this manipulation of audiences as a way of generating and manipulating the internal dialogue that transpires as one writes, and I claim that this is another aspect of Elbow's dialogic pedagogy. Even though Elbow himself resists the idea that all private writing is social and therefore dialogic, I will argue that private writing is always a social dialogue with the "audience of self" and that it is a far more enabling metaphor for writers than Elbow's concept of nonaudience.

In "Closing My Eyes As I Speak," Elbow wishes to counter rather pervasive calls for pedagogies that advocate making students more aware of audience and he wishes to celebrate "the benefits of ignoring audience" (50). He claims,

> It's not that writers should never think about their audience. It's a question of when. An audience is a field of force. The closer we come—the more we think about these readers—the stronger the pull they exert on the contents of our minds. The practical question, then, is always whether a particular audience functions as a helpful field of force or one that confuses or inhibits us. (51)

Elbow is concerned that the increased attention paid in composition pedagogy to issues of audience and purpose will lead students into problems that, he argues, can best be addressed by moving away from concepts of audience that can inhibit or distort writing. In making this argument, he reiterates a claim he makes in *Writing With Power* that it is possible *not* to write to an audience at all, a concept of writing for a *nonaudience*. In fact, there are two kinds of nonaudience:

> *Safe Nonaudience.* When you write for no one—for the wastebasket, for yourself, for the process itself—words often come pouring out of you. You find new voices, sounds, and tones.
>
> *Dangerous Nonaudience.* But when you feel you have no real audience at all—no one who cares what is on your mind either immediately or in the future—you are likely to drift into dull muteness: to feel as though you have

nothing to say, nothing on you mind, no thoughts to share. (*Writing With Power* 188)

Elbow claims that private (as opposed to public) writing can be directed to no one and without communicative intent. In other words, he claims there are situations in which no type of dialogue occurs with the self. It is my contention that the very concept of nonaudience can be disabling to students and that the metaphor of "audience of self"—a concept close to Elbow's safe nonaudience—is more enabling.

Elbow is well aware of the arguments against the concept of truly private writing that does not address an audience, and he attempts to meet these arguments head on in "Closing My Eyes As I Speak":

> Some readers who see *all* discourse as social will object to my opposition between public and private writing (the "trap of oppositional thinking") and insist that *there is no such thing as private discourse.* What looks like private, solitary mental work, they would say, is really social. (61)

He even seems to talk himself into agreeing with his socially minded critics:

> Even if "private writing" is "deep down" social, the fact remains that, as we engage in it, we don't have to worry about whether it works on readers or even makes sense. We can refrain from doing all the things that audience-awareness advocates advise us to do ("keeping our audience in mind as we write" and trying to "decenter"). Therefore this social–discourse theory doesn't undermine the benefits of "private writing" and thus provides no support at all for the traditional rhetorical advice that we should "always

try to think about (intended) audience as we write."

In fact this social-discourse theory reinforces two subsidiary arguments I have been making. First, even if there is no getting away from *some* audience, we can get relief from an inhibiting audience by writing to a more inviting one. Second, audience problems don't come only from *actual* audiences but also from phantom "audiences in the head" (Elbow, *Writing With Power* 186ff). Once we learn how to be more aware of the effects of both external and internal readers and how to direct our words elsewhere, we can get out of the shadow even of a troublesome phantom reader. (62)

He realizes that social–discourse theory works in many ways to bolster his claims. However, even in the face of all the support that he himself garners, he cannot abandon the distinction between public and private writing and the possibility of nonaudience.

Elbow agrees that there are times when private writing is addressed to an audience of self, but he also insists that there are situations when it is "*not* communication with audience of self" (63). He describes two such situations:

Freewriting to no one: for the *sake* of the self but not *to* the self. The goal is not to communicate but to follow a train of thinking or feeling to see where it leads. In doing this kind of freewriting (and many people have not learned it), you don't particularly plan to come back and read what you've written. You just write along and the written product falls away to be ignored, while the only "real product"—any new perceptions, thoughts, or feelings produced in the mind by the freewriting—is saved and looked at again. (It's not that you don't experience your words *at all* but you experience them as speaker, sender, or emitter—not as receiver or audience. To say that's the same as being audience is denying the very distinction between 'speaker' and 'audience'.)

Writing as exorcism is a more extreme example of private writing *not* for the audience of self. Some people have learned to write in order to get rid of thoughts or feeling. By freewriting what's obsessively going round and round in our head we can finally let it go and move on. (63)

To say that there is no communicative intention in this kind of writing is to make a false distinction that "communication" is always directed to someone other than the speaker. Communicative intention in this case, "the goal," is communication with the self; it is to communicate where a train of thought or feeling leads, which is a valid rhetorical purpose often used in exploratory discourse.

I would not agree that in arguing for an internal listener, or reader, one denies the distinction between "speaker" and "audience," but, rather, that the distinction, borrowed from oral rhetoric, is certainly already blurred in any writing situation. In any writing situation, the writer carries *some* concept of audience. It is entirely reasonable to posit that in private writing the self establishes its own audience demands, demands so enabling that they seem to disappear but remain necessary if we are to speak *even to ourselves*. It seems more a matter of degree than of an either/or: "audience of self" or "nonaudience." Even in Elbow's extreme example of "writing as exorcism" (which is not a discourse form appropriate for college–level composition classrooms), the self listens to itself as it pours out words. Try not listening while you are putting words on a page, even if the page is concealed from sight or the computer monitor is turned off. A listener, even for the most personal of prose, is projected in much the same way that the other audiences are characterized within the imagination. What is finally more important is not which theoretical terms you prefer but which are more enabling to writers. In the following I agree with Elbow:

> As teachers, particularly, we need to distinguish and emphasize "private writing" in order to teach it, to teach that crucial cognitive capacity to engage in extended and productive thinking that doesn't depend on audience prompts or social stimuli. It's sad to see so many students who can reply to live voices but cannot engage in productive dialogue with the voices in their heads. Such students often lose interest in an issue that had intrigued them—just because they don't find other people who are interested in talking about it and haven't learned to talk reflectively to *themselves* about it. (62)

This is exactly the reason why conceiving private writing as not having any audience or addressee can trick a writer into the lair of the "dangerous nonaudience," of finding no internal listener to engage in dialogue when he or she sits down to freewrite. Instead, it seems much more productive to encourage the writer to conceive of private writing as a dialogue with concepts of self and to envision rhetorical situations where he or she can be in complete control. The free play of creating many enabling audiences seems infinitely more useful to a writer than Elbow's seemingly empty term *nonaudience*. The catch is that sometimes the self is motivated to listen and sometimes it is not (for various reasons: sometimes the words are threatening to the self; sometimes they are not valued by the self and then get censored). It is not that we need a nonaudience; on the contrary, we need a listener—sometimes one that seems not to be listening—one that is so quiet that it may seem like a nonaudience, but *some* self has to hear in order to record the words. It is simply a matter of degree.

Ultimately, Elbow's pedagogy is about developing internal dialogues. The dialogues that transpire in the classroom are meant to develop an internal mechanism that then guides the process as the student writes alone. When a writer manipulates audience concepts, he or she is also managing a process of internal and enabling dialogues.

Expressivist Dialogics

As has been demonstrated, dialogic pedagogy can have different goals and therefore different outcomes. Macrorie and Elbow, for instance, the dialogic group "stands in" for the future "real" audiences, providing immediate feedback to the writer. However, Murray's dialogic group is primarily interested in responding to the student's process, that is, to the activities that he or she is engaged in so as to produce the written product. The dialogue only addresses the written text as it reflects accurately or inaccurately the writer's notion of what it is. Murray's dialogue is not about the quality or effect of a written document in process but about the writer's awareness of the document and the process of producing it.

Unlike the social constructionists, radical pedagogy theorists, or poststructuralists discussed in the next three chapters, the expressivists have a uniquely personal concept of dialogism. They are concerned with dialogic interaction with others only insofar as such interaction helps to promote the writer's ability to dialogue more effectively with the inner self and thereby come to know that inner self. In effect, social dialogue is secondary and subordinate to dialogue with the self. Expressivist composition theory does not emphasize the *social* dialogic nature of writing, does not envision writing as part of a larger conversation that is carried on in social groups. Expressivists see the act of writing as ultimately a lonely task that is best performed on one's own—away from the contamination of too many other voices that will obscure what the writer truly needs to say. As Elbow says in the opening of *Sharing and Responding*: "We talk in company, we write alone" (1).

Because of the expressivists' emphasis on self-knowledge and self-expression, they are not interested in dialogue as social interaction or in seeing written discourse first as an attempt to communicate with others. They are only interested in dialogic social interaction as it elicits from the writer the "truth" of the self's unique experience of the world. In giving new writers opportunities to engage in self dialogue, they promote internal dialogues that allow students access to that knowledge and the critical awareness to observe when that experience is authentic.

In a sense, the expressivists are making a political statement. They see a danger in the personal not being fully explored and expressed. According to expressivists, writing is always in danger of expressing "lies." Macrorie's goal is "truthtelling" in student writing because "good" writing is defined precisely as that which "tells the truth." Murray writes, "The writer doesn't . . . look to the audience first and write down what the reader wants to hear" ("Interior View" 11). He is implying that if a writer composes for another, the writer may be tempted to tell others what they want to hear and ignore the truth. Elbow, too, is suspect of audience: "An audience is a field of force. The closer we come—the more we think about these readers—the stronger the pull they exert on the contents of our minds" ("Closing My Eyes" 51). Audiences have the potential to drive a writer away from truth, unless they are managed properly. The goal is always to discover and express the authenticity of personal existence. Of course, Elbow does stress more than

Macrorie and Murray that writing should, at some point, become social—be published and read, get "into other people's heads." The question is simply *when* this happens; he wants to make sure that the *personal* vision is allowed to develop first.

I should note too, if it is not already apparent, that there is a real contradiction or tension in expressivist theory between the public and private, self and other, and theory and practice. Ironically, expressivists use dialogic pedagogies that involve social interaction but claim that writing is primarily an act of self-discovery, not communication. Yet, they believe that the most effective way of coming to know one's self is in a supportive group of others. These contradictions have yet to be resolved, though many scholars are beginning to look much more closely at expressivist scholarship.[6]

In chapter two, I discuss a group of theorists who advocate teaching methods similar to the expressivists but who envision the writing process itself as a social activity in which any particular piece of writing is already part of a larger conversation that is ultimately involved with others in making sense of the world, in "making meaning" rather than merely recording it.

Notes

1. See Berlin and Faigley.

2. Although there is much student discussion described in the work of Coles, the purpose of the discussion is Coles' own "enactment" of acceptable discourse. The subject of the course is the relationship of language, experience, and individual identity. Coles tries to perform for the students the proper way to view writing. Coles' view of the text is the "correct" one, and the students are led through the discussion to see things his way. They do not respond to

each other's writing, nor is there much emphasis on writing as a transaction between audience and writer. Although Donald Stewart advocates prewriting, his textbook does not emphasize interaction.

3. Note the similarity to Freire's concept of "banking" education, discussed in detail in chapter three.

4. According to Lindemann, Macrorie began experimenting with freewriting while still a graduate student at the University of North Carolina. See "Ken Macrorie" 362.

5. As I will discuss in chapter three, the element of building trust in order to maintain dialogue is an important issue in Freirean theory and radical pedagogy in general.

6. See Harris.

Social Constructionism
and Dialogism

As I discussed in the previous chapter, expressivist rhetoric assumes that all "good" writing springs from the individual. The writer's task is to look inward in order to interpret the world; writing is a personal matter. The expressivists were highly influential in composition studies throughout the 1970s and early 1980s; however, they have increasingly come under attack by those composition scholars who subscribe to a "social" view of writing and epistemology. These compositionists have been influenced largely by an epistemological movement most often called "social constructionism." The social constructionists have become the most powerful and influential force in composition scholarship, and a "social–epistemic" view of writing, language, and epistemology pervades much recent scholarship. This social view of writing is thoroughly dialogic in conception.

Social Construction and the Justification of Belief

Social construction is an epistemology that maintains that knowledge is a product of social interaction. That is, what we call "knowledge" is the product of negotiation and consensus among members of a discourse community. Knowledge is no longer seen as something external to human beings, existing apart from social interaction, available to be "discovered." Kenneth A. Bruffee writes:

> A social constructionist position in any discipline assumes
> that entities we normally call reality, knowledge, thought,
> facts, texts, selves, and so on are constructs generated by
> communities of like-minded peers. Social construction
> understands reality, knowledge, thought, facts, texts, selves,
> and so on as community-generated and community-
> maintained linguistic entities—or, more broadly speaking,
> symbolic entities—that define or "constitute" the
> communities that generate them. ("Social Construction"
> 774)

Rather than viewing knowledge as something discovered "out
there" in the "real" world through empirical methods, social
constructionists argue that facts, the self, "reality," and even
knowledge itself are constructed through a dialectical interaction
among language, culture, people, and the material world.

The social constructionist perspective derives in part from
the work of Thomas Kuhn, who argues in his now-famous
Structure of Scientific Revolutions that contrary to popular
belief, scientific knowledge is not a product of scientists'
coming increasingly closer to "truth." Rather, scientific knowledge is a product of consensus within the scientific community;
that is, knowledge is created, not found. Kuhn argued that
scientists think and work within commonly held intellectual
frameworks, or "paradigms," and new knowledge results when
the current paradigm no longer satisfactorily explains certain
phenomena. Scientists then search for and create a new
explanatory paradigm. If the new paradigm seems a reasonable
alternative to the old one, so much so that members of the
scientific community consensually agree to replace the old
with the new, then a "scientific revolution" has occurred.
Thus, scientific knowledge often comes about through revolution, not evolution as is commonly supposed.

Drawing on Kuhn's ground-breaking work, philosopher Richard Rorty has extended the notion of knowledge being a product of consensus. Rorty contends that *all* knowledge, not just scientific knowledge, is created by members of specific communities who agree that one thing is true and another false. In a devastating critique of Western metaphysics and analytical philosophy, Rorty denies the centuries-old belief that intellectual history is a continual building on a foundation of verifiable truth, that we are coming closer and closer to truly "knowing" the world. Instead, Rorty adopts the "anti-foundationalist" position that no such foundation exists or ever can. Rather than being eternal and unshakable, knowledge is a temporary and contingent construct: bound in particular times and places, something that helps us cope with the world for the time being—until we replace this knowledge with a more "useful" construct.

Clearly, Kuhn's and Rorty's notion of knowledge being constructed through consensus means that both discourse and dialogue take on primary importance. No longer is language seen as a conduit through which we transmit thoughts and knowledge; rather, language becomes *constitutive* of knowledge itself. In effect, all knowledge is rhetorical, a product of discourse. Only through a process of dialogue, negotiation, and consensus building does knowledge come about. One can also say, then, that all knowledge is dialogic, or at least that it is a product of dialogism. In fact, as I will soon discuss, the metaphor often used for this dialogic process is "conversation."

Several assumptions differentiate social constructionism from "cognitive epistemology," which itself is largely derived from Descartes. In traditional Cartesian thinking, "there must be a universal foundation, a ground, a base, a framework, a structure of some sort behind knowledge or beneath it, upon which what we know is built, assuring its certainty or truth" (Bruffee,

"Social Construction" 776). This foundation is used to measure the truth value of knowledge; for example, superstitions
might be measured against the foundation of the word of God.
In the context of this discussion, in expressivist rhetoric, truth
value is measured against the assumed foundation of the
individual's inner vision of the world. In contrast, social
constructionists deny any such foundation for the structure of
knowledge. Instead, "There is only an agreement, a consensus
arrived at for the time being by communities of knowledgeable
peers" (777).

A second assumption is that the mind functions in certain
universal modes, that certain modes of thinking are innate,
"objectifiable, and perhaps even measurable entities" in the
"black box" of the mind (777). Rather, social construction
assumes that thinking is not a product of the mind per se but
is an *internalized version of conversation*. In other words,
thought is already social in nature, springing from the social
activity of conversation, or dialogue, internalized.

Third, cognitivist epistemology assumes that "the individual
self is the matrix of all thought: 'I think, therefore I am.'" In
contrast, social construction assumes that

> the matrix of thought is not the individual self but some
> community of knowledgeable peers and the vernacular
> language of that community. That is, social construction
> understands knowledge and the authority of knowledge
> as community-generated, community-maintaining
> symbolic artifacts. (777)

Similarly, the concept of a self as discrete and autonomous is
denied in social constructionist theory. Instead, the self is
understood to be socially constructed by its interaction with
the personal and cultural contexts with which it must learn to

cope. In social construction theory, the self is created in a dialectic with the social group.

The most important assumption that social constructionists make, especially for composition studies, is that knowledge and language are inseparable. Cognitivist epistemology has viewed language as the medium or conduit for thought—the dress of one's thoughts—therefore positioning language on the margins of knowledge. But, as Bruffee argues, social constructionism understands that language and knowledge are identical, placing language and rhetoric at the center of attempts to understand knowledge and its authority ("Social Construction" 778).

Clearly, social constructionists understand language to be a *social* activity. As Kenneth A. Gergen points out, "Languages are essentially shared activities. Indeed, until the sounds or markings come to be shared within a community, it is inappropriate to speak of language at all" (270). Language, whether written or spoken, private or public, is not a thing in itself but an activity that two or more people who share some social connections engage in together; language does not exist until it is, at least, dialogue.

Composition theorists who draw on social constructionist epistemology, conceive of the writer's task as interacting with language, other people, and culture and that through that interaction, knowledge is "made" and maintained. In this view, writing is a purely social activity. Not only is writing thought of as an activity that involves collaboration with others, but also written documents themselves are understood as part of social interactions, as parts in a series of ongoing dialogues or conversations within and among communities or groups of people; documents are no longer thought of as autonomous utterances unconnected to other documents and people. Writing is no longer seen as a simple one-way transferral of information from one person to others but as part of a dialogue in which authors *and* readers produce and maintain knowledge. In composition scholarship, this view of writing is often called the "social constructionist" or "social-epistemic" perspective.

Marilyn Cooper's Ecological Model

Some composition theorists have begun to work out the implications of social-epistemic views of writing in more concrete ways, developing models that help students and instructors understand more fully what it means to say that writing is a social activity. One of the first of these exploratory models is Marilyn M. Cooper's "ecological" model. She is reacting against the limited view of writing that sees the "ideal" writer as

> isolated from the social world, a writer I will call the solitary author. The solitary author works alone, within the privacy of his own mind. He uses free writing exercises and heuristics to find out what he knows about a subject and to find something he wants to say to others; he uses his analytic skills to discover a purpose, to imagine an audience, to decide on strategies, to organize content; and he simulates how his text will be read by reading it over himself, making the final revisions necessary to assure its success when he abandons it to the world of which he is not a part. (4)

In contrast, a social or ecological view of writing includes more than an individual writer and his or her immediate surroundings. Like the natural ecological systems described in the biological sciences, writing is envisioned as a highly interconnected and dynamic system in which all actions affect all other actions. To describe the composing situation, Cooper uses the metaphor of a web "in which anything that affects one strand of the web vibrates throughout the whole" (9). Any move by any writer changes the relationship of the systems and in turn changes the writer's situation. Cooper emphasizes that these "systems" do not comprise a series of finite categories but a "web" of systems that are "made and remade by writers in the act of writing" (7). These systems are also influenced by other larger and dynamic cultural and historical forces that change over longer periods of time. Furthermore, while these systems are, in "real time," always changing, they can still be specified at any given time.

Cooper identifies five of these interacting systems. The *system of ideas* is "the means by which writers comprehend their world" in order to transform "individual experiences and observations into knowledge." The process by which writers interact with ideas is a dialogic one. Cooper argues that ideas result from face-to-face contact with texts. The dialogic process that results in ideas is "continuous"; the process is ongoing as long as members of the community continue to engage in dialogue. It is not necessarily dependent on any single member and can last over many generations, although what is talked about will change over time (8).

The *system of purposes* describes what is accomplished in the communal dialogue or, as Cooper writes, it is "the means by which writers coordinate their actions." For example, "arguments attempt to set agendas; promises attempt to set schedules and relationships"; and so on. Like ideas, the purposes of the dialogue emanate from the interaction. Individuals' purposes and those of the group modify each other; indeed, as Cooper explains, "an individual impulse or need only becomes a purpose when it is recognized as such by others" (8).

The *system of interpersonal interactions* is the "means by which writers regulate their access to one another." In other words, it is the system that specifies who is sanctioned to talk to whom. This system makes itself manifest in certain overt and covert ways, such as in "chains of command" and other institutional hierarchies that regulate the etiquette of dialogue in certain situations. The two factors that govern the way in which writers interact with others are "intimacy, a measure of closeness based on similarity seen to be relevant—kinship, religion, occupation; and power, a measure of the degree to which a writer can control the action of others" (8). In other words, dialogue is sanctioned by the social relationship of the conversants and by the power individual speakers or groups are perceived to possess. For example, it is often argued that white males in Western culture are sanctioned to engage in dialogue in more situations than are women, children, or people of color,.

What Cooper calls the *system of cultural norms* determines the role one plays in the dialogue. As Cooper explains, "One always writes out of a group." Writers' roles derive from the larger organizational, social structures of cultural norms embodied in institutions like universities, the professions, or business, whether one writes in the role of academic scholar or student, scientist, or accountant. As in all aspects of an ecological system, the system of cultural norms both constructs the roles for writers and is in turn constructed by writers as they interact with the system (8–9).

The fifth system that Cooper isolates is the *system of textual forms*, that is, "the means by which writers communicate." Textual forms must remain stable enough to be comprehensible, yet be flexible enough to be adapted to many different purposes. Thus, textual forms are both "conservative" and "revolutionary" means of action (8–9).

Cooper's model foregrounds the importance of dialogue and other rhetorical activities. Discourse production is no longer perceived as sending a one–way message to a reader. In social constructionist theory, writer and reader are seen as conversing or engaging in a dialogue that is affected by many social forces. Cooper asserts that to envision writing ecologically is to see it as constructing and constructive of interactive systems in which the author and audience are related social beings, not "remote images: an author, an audience" (12).

A Social Theory of Rhetoric

Perhaps even more influential than Cooper's work in furthering the social–epistemic perspective in composition is Karen Burke LeFevre's *Invention as a Social Act*. LeFevre formulates a rhetorical theory that accounts for the social aspects of writing. Although her monograph is ostensibly about "invention," invention serves as a synecdoche for rhetoric itself. LeFevre argues that viewing invention in the narrow Platonic sense, with its focus on individual "introspective self–examination," is inadequate and has limited our understanding of the role of invention and, therefore, of rhetoric itself (11). Invention, defined by LeFevre in broad terms, is "the process of actively creating as well as finding what comes to be known and said in the discourse of any discipline," and it occurs "when individuals interact dialectically with socioculture in a distinctive way to generate something" (33). She overtly links rhetorical invention to the more common meaning of invention as the "creation of something new," and closely associates invention with inquiry. Rhetorical invention, as LeFevre interprets it, is the process of producing discourse.

She identifies "several significant social aspects of invention":

- The inventing "self" is socially influenced, even socially constituted.

- One invents with language or with other symbol systems, which are socially created and shared by members of discourse communities.

- Invention builds on a foundation of knowledge accumulated from previous generations, knowledge that constitutes a social legacy of ideas, forms, and ways of thinking.

- Invention may be enabled by an internal dialogue with an imagined other or a construct of audience that supplies premises or structures of belief guiding the inventor.

- Writers often invent by involving other people: as editors and evaluators . . . as "resonators" . . . as collaborators . . . and as opponents or devil's advocates.

- Invention is powerfully influenced by social collectives, such as institutions, bureaucracies, governments, and "invisible colleges" of academic disciplinary communities.

- The reception, evaluation, and use of what is invented depend to a great extent on social context. (33–35)

The Platonic view, which is closely related (if not identical) to the expressivist view discussed in chapter one, is unable to accommodate these features of the production of discourse because it is, according to LeFevre, an "incomplete view."

The Platonic perspective has contributed greatly to our understanding of the role of invention in composing and to "encouraging reflection"; however, it has restricted our understanding of invention significantly: "It leads us to study the individual inventor apart from sociocultural contexts; it depicts invention as a closed, one–way system, and the inventor as an atomistic unit, abstracted from society; and it fails to acknowledge that invention is often a collaborative process" (32).

LeFevre has devised a four–part continuum of perspectives on invention that can be employed as a theoretical framework to understand the social nature of invention. On one end of the continuum is the *Platonic perspective*, which "concerns invention as a private, asocial activity engaged in by an individual who possesses innate knowledge to be recollected and expressed, or innate cognitive structures to be projected onto the world" (49–50). This perspective is largely assumed in the expressivist view held by such theorists as Elbow, Macrorie, and Murray.

Internal dialogic is the second perspective. As discussed in chapter one, expressivists such as Elbow and Murray employ pedagogical strategies that involve internal dialogue, but their concept of internal dialogue still centers on the individual's writing process and does not acknowledge the social aspects of internal dialogue (although Elbow's recent work seems to be moving in that direction). The social view of internal dialogic "maintains that invention is largely a process of internal dialogue or dialectic with another 'self,' often involving internalized constructs influenced by external social forces and actual people" (50). Although LeFevre bases her explanation of internal dialogue on Freud's concept of "superego," many social theorists rely heavily on Russian psychologist Lev Vygotsky's concept of "inner speech" to explain the social nature of internal dialogue, as I will demonstrate later in this chapter.

The *collaborative perspective* maintains that "people interact to invent and to create a resonating environment for inventors" (50). LeFevre elaborates:

Whether a writer interacts with those whose roles are advisory, or collaborates with others who are equally responsible for the outcome, there is in either case an emphasis on transactions between people and on adjustive responses . . . on the part of both writers and readers. Something new comes about because of the ways people act with each other; inventions do not occur solely in the mind of an independent actor. (63)

This view of invention has become the most dominant social perspective and informs much of Bruffee's work.

On the other end of the continuum from the Platonic perspective is the *collective perspective*. From this view, "invention is neither a purely individual nor an interpersonal act or process; rather, it is encouraged or constrained by social collectives whose views are transmitted through such things as institutions, societal prohibitions, and cultural expectations" (50). What is interesting about this conception of invention is that it allows us to appreciate the constraints as well as the motivations that arise due to the influence of large social units. According to LeFevre:

Expectations of society, attitudes fostered by institutions, funding preferences of public and private agencies, tacit rules about the nature of evidence and procedures for inquiry, and availability of equipment and materials— these are but a few examples of what influences our inventions. Forces exerted by social collectives prohibit some inventions and promote others. (78)

LeFevre's work is the first "to draw together major work in philosophy, interpretive theory, social psychology, and composition pedagogy in the service of an argument for seeing invention as socially situated" (Bizzell 485). In LeFevre's view, invention is influenced by a number of dialogues, from those carried on internally with socially constructed other selves to those carried on with larger social entities that rely on discourse in order to function on a daily basis.

In LeFevre's formulation, invention, and rhetoric itself, is a thoroughly dialogic activity—dialogue that involves many participants and that creates knowledge as it is engaged in by discourse communities. LeFevre's rhetorical theory clearly locates the writer in expansive socio–cultural contexts. Once we acknowledge all the ways that writers do, in fact, interact with a variety of "others," we can no longer abstract writers from the social contexts that motivate and influence discourse production. Rather than the "incomplete view" of discourse production presented in the expressivist view, LeFevre provides composition studies with a much broader account of the composing process, one in which interaction and dialogue are essential.

Writing Group Theory

Perhaps the most important and visible way that social-epistemic composition theory has influenced our notions of rhetoric and dialogue is through writing group theory and scholarship on collaborative learning. Anne Ruggles Gere notes that writing instructors seem to keep rediscovering writing groups when actually they have been employed, even if marginally, since colonial times (9). She documents a steady stream of scholarship on the subject from 1880 to 1985 (125–43). It is only recently that writing groups have become a dominant and important aspect of how writing is taught in U.S. schools. And it is only recently that theorists have begun to provide theoretical support for their use in teaching writing. Gere offers a rationale for why writing groups are effective in teaching writing.

Gere hypothesizes that writers had become alienated from their audiences and language because of composition theory's focus on individual writers and the writer's individuality. She outlines cultural and historical trends that have led to the common view of writers as solitary individuals who create out of themselves. For instance, in the sixteenth century copyright was granted to publishers, not authors. At that time, writers were considered artisans who manipulated the rules of rhetoric and poetics, and their work was considered public property. Copyright was not legally granted to authors until the eighteenth century, as early as 1710 in England. In the nineteenth century, Romantic poets proclaimed the "centrality of the writer's perception," contrary to the long–standing notion that a piece of writing is judged by the "degree of pleasure" in the audience, a notion that M.H. Abrams argues can be traced as far back as Horace (60). Until recently, literary theory followed the lead of Romantic poets and has focused largely on the notion of the individual literary genius (65).

These neo–Romantic notions are currently being replaced by a social–epistemic view of writing and of writing pedagogy. Collaboration, Gere claims, helps students overcome their alienation from their audience by "reorienting them" toward readers. The long hiatus in our thinking about reading and writing as social acts has left them without adequate frameworks to view writing as communicating with others. Collaborative learning employed in the writing classroom helps students make a fundamental shift in their view of writing away from the stereotype of the isolated genius to a communicative, dialogic view. As Gere explains:

> The peer who says "I don't understand" establishes—more powerfully than any theory, instructor's exhortation, or written comment can— the "otherness" of the audience and pushes writers to respond to this otherness by searching for more effective ways to convey ideas. (68)

Gere also cites evidence that a significant number of English speakers in the United States suffer anxiety about the way they speak and are alienated from their language as well as from readers. Gere offers the collaborative group as a way for these students to explore language within a linguistic community whose language habits and skill level are similar, thereby gaining a new intimacy with language as they talk with others and read aloud.

According to Gere, certain necessary conditions need to be met in the collaborative groups if alienation is to be truly overcome: "Collaboration that effectively reduces alienation appears in groups where not one individual constantly dominates, where all members are supported, and where individual contributions are developed upon by other members" (68-69). Moreover, collaboration alone is not enough for learning to take place in the groups either:

> While the democratic give–and–take of collaboration is essential, it does not by itself guarantee that any learning will take place. Participants in collaborative groups learn when they challenge one another with questions, when they use the edidence and information available to them, when they develop relationships among issues, when they

evaluate their own thinking. In other words, they learn when they assume that knowledge is something they can help create rather than something to be received whole from someone else. (69)

Clearly, collaborative groups offer students close proximity to audiences—an opportunity to engage in dialogue with readers—and opportunities to explore language by using it in dialogic situations. Like the expressivists, social theorists understand the importance of immediate feedback to beginning writers. However, unlike expressivist theory, Gere's theory of the purpose and function of writing groups assumes that writing is a social activity and that knowledge is also generated and maintained by groups of people with similar interests. Thus, writing group theory reinforces and enacts social constructionism in composition pedagogy by positioning writers to interact dialogically so as to create their own knowledge and to help provide them the social conditions that foster reconciliation with writers, readers, and language. In fact, it is through writing group theory that Bruffee developed his now–famous theoretical rationale for collaborative learning and peer tutoring.

Kenneth Bruffee and the "Conversation of Mankind"

No one has done more to promote social constructionism and collaborative learning in composition studies than Kenneth Bruffee. As Bruffee outlines in "Collaborative Learning and the 'Conversation of Mankind,'" many college–level instructors turned to various forms of dialogic pedagogy—what Bruffee calls collaborative learning—in the 1970s out of "pressing educational need." For a variety of reasons but primarily because of open admissions, college–level instructors were faced with a significant number of students who were either underprepared or for other reasons were unable to adjust to the conventions of postsecondary education (637). After some experimentation, compositionists found that these students responded better to help from their peers than to institution-sponsored tutoring that simply mirrored the same conventions that the students were having trouble with. Bruffee discovered a precedent for these procedures first in the research of several British secondary school instructors who were concerned with "democratizing education and to eliminating from education what were perceived then as socially destructive authoritarian social forms," and second in the work of M.L.K. Abercrombie, who found that medical students working in collaborative groups learned medical judgment faster and better than students working alone (636)[7]. As Bruffee concludes, "Collaborative learning, it seemed, harnessed the powerful educative force of peer influence that had been—and largely still is—ignored and hence wasted by traditional forms of education" (638).

But many instructors find that in practice, collaborative learning does not always work. In an effort to help them improve practice, Bruffee attempts to provide instructors with a conceptual rationale. Much of his rationale is derived from social constructionist epistemology, which, as noted earlier, sees all knowledge as constructed dialogically by groups of socially interacting people. Bruffee makes a connection between dialogue, thought, and knowledge, arguing that it is through "conversation" that all knowledge is constructed. Bruffee draws heavily on Michael Oakeshott, who writes:

As civilized human beings, we are the inheritors, neither of an inquiry about ourselves and the world, nor of an accumulating body of information, but of a conversation, begun in the primeval forests and extended and made

more articulate in the course of centuries. It is a conversation which goes on both in public and within each of ourselves.
... Education, properly speaking, is an initiation into the skill and partnership of this conversation in which we learn to recognize the voices, to distinguish the proper occasions of utterance, and in which we acquire the intellectual and moral habits appropriate to conversation. And it is this conversation which, in the end, gives place and character to every human activity and utterance. (Oakeshott, qtd. in Bruffee, "Conversation" 638–39)

Oakeshott draws attention to the crucial relationship between thought and dialogue. What we have inherited is a dialogue that is both public and private, both among individuals and groups of individuals as well as within ourselves. This internal dialogue is often called "reflective thought." First, as children, we learn to converse with others; later, as we mature, we internalize these conversations as thought. In short, we displace social conversations by performing them silently to ourselves as thought.

Therefore, because thought is internalized conversation, thought and conversation largely tend to work the same way. Bruffee argues:

To the extent that thought is internalized conversation, then, any effort to understand how we think requires us to understand the nature of conversation; and any effort to understand conversation requires us to understand the nature of community life that generates and maintains conversation. Furthermore, any effort to understand and cultivate in ourselves the kind of thought we value most requires us to understand and cultivate the kinds of community life that establish and maintain conversation that is the origin of that kind of thought. To think well as individuals we must learn to think well collectively— that is, we must learn to converse well. The first steps to learning to think better, therefore, are learning to converse better and learning to establish and maintain the sorts of social context, the sorts of community life, that foster the sort of conversation members of the community value. (640)

Because thinking and dialogue are closely related, Bruffee argues, the social context of the classroom needs to reflect the social relationships that generate and maintain knowledge. Since knowledge, in this view, is not located in the minds of experts but in the *conversations* of experts, then the task of education is to provide the opportunity for students to talk— to engage in these knowledge–producing and maintaining conversations.

The social constructivist view of knowledge, thought, and dialogue has significant implications for composition instructors. As Bruffee maintains, "If thought is internalized conversation, then writing is internalized conversation re–externalized." Bruffee explains,

Like thought, writing is related to conversation in both time and function. Writing is a technologically displaced form of conversation. When we write, having already internalized the "skill and partnership" of conversation, we displace it once more onto the written page. But because thought is already one step away from conversation, the position of writing relative to conversation is more complex than the position of thought relative to conversation. Writing is at once two steps away from conversation and a return to conversation. We

converse; we internalize conversation as thought; and
then by writing, we re-immerse conversation in its
external, social medium. (641)

In short, writing returns thought to its social context.

The goal then for instructors is to provide contexts in the
classroom in which students can engage in dialogue among
themselves and with other discourse communities through
reading and writing. Students need to talk about ideas as a way
of fostering thinking about ideas, and then in turn they need to
write about ideas as a way of joining in the dialogue. This
classroom dialogue should be similar to the conversations that
college instructors (as representatives of the various academic
and professional communities to which the students aspire)
value. Bruffee argues that

> our task must involve engaging students in conversation
> among themselves at as many points in both the writing
> and the reading process as possible, and that we should
> contrive to ensure that students' conversation about what
> they read and write is similar in as many ways as possible
> to the way we would like them eventually to read and
> write. The way they talk with each other determines the
> way they will think and the way they will write. (642)

In this way the classroom becomes an approximation of the
dialogic contexts that students will encounter when they leave
school. The classroom is designed as a microcosm of the larger
communities that the students will eventually join. Students
learn by engaging in dialogue with a community of status-
equal peers to model the kinds of discourse that are valued by
the larger society. They also learn by engaging in "displaced
conversations," by reading and writing texts that serve as

"stand-ins" for actual conversation transpiring in real communities. Reading, writing, and talking, all understood as ways people interact or as dialogue, are what foster learning.

Bruffee argues that the primary task of composition instructors is to teach "normal discourse," a term he borrows from Rorty who in turn fashioned it after a concept of Kuhn's. According to Bruffee, "Normal discourse . . . applies to conversation within a community of knowledgeable peers. A community of knowledgeable peers is a group of people who accept, and whose work is guided by, the same paradigms and the same code of values and assumptions" (642). Normal discourse includes the conventions of what is commonly thought of as "standard English" but also refers to those rhetorical conventions, patterns of thought, and agreed upon assumptions that are commonly used by particular groups of people. For example, legal discourse has different rhetorical conventions, patterns of thought, and agreed upon assumptions than the discourse of psychology; even though one could find places where these discourse communities intersect, each has recognizable discourse conventions. Moreover, the purpose of normal discourse is to justify belief to the satisfaction of other people within the author's community of knowledgeable peers.

By learning to use these accepted forms and rhetorical conventions, students come to identify themselves as members of particular discourse communities: biologists, mathematicians, historians, accountants, literary critics, and so on. As Bruffee argues, "This is so because to be conversant with the normal discourse in a field of study or endeavor is exactly what we mean by being knowledgeable—that is, knowledge-able— in that field. . . . Mastery of a knowledge community's normal discourse is the basic qualification for acceptance into that community" (643).

Inevitably, an important question arises: how can students who are not members of knowledge communities and who are deficient in the knowledge of particular communities help each other enter the conversations of new communities? Bruffee provides two answers to this question. First, students already belong to numerous discourse communities; they already have a notion, no matter how ill-formed, of what written discourse is like. When students pool the resources they learned indirectly by mastering the conversation of other discourse communities, and when they direct those resources toward a "judiciously designed" task that involves interaction with the new discourse community and that builds on the knowledge that students already have, learning can be significantly enhanced. Of course, judiciously designing tasks for students is no easy matter, as I will discuss later.

The second answer is central to social constructionist theory itself. If we accept the premise that knowledge is socially constructed by a community of knowledgeable peers using the language conventions of that community and that learning is a social rather than an individual process, then learning is not assimilating information but rather a social and collaborative effort to create and maintain knowledge. In this way students explain to themselves and others why a particular way of understanding is preferable to another. As Bruffee contends:

> We establish knowledge or justify belief collaboratively by challenging each other's biases, and presuppositions; by negotiating collectively toward new paradigms of perception, thought, feeling, and expression; and by joining larger, more experienced communities of knowledgeable peers through assenting to those communities' interests, values, language, and paradigms of perceptions and thought. (646)

In this model, students are reacculturated into the communities they aspire to.[2] By practicing the normal discourse of a particular field, members are able to engage in dialogue or converse with other members of the field even though they are displaced by time and space; through this dialogic process they become participants in the knowledge maintaining and producing activities of various communities.

Bruffee sees this negotiation of knowledge as primarily a one–way process; the goal is to impart the social conventions of the knowledge communities and institutions to the students. Students make themselves over into acceptable members of the new discourse communities. There is very little emphasis on what knowledge communities do to accommodate or discourage new members. In contrast, Freirean theory, discussed in chapter three, understands that if education is to be liberatory and not merely indoctrinary, it must involve conciliatory change in both the discourse community and those who aspire to join its dialogues.

Thinking of writing as a social activity rather than as a personal one brings writing, thinking, and dialogue into "constructive" relation. Understanding writing and learning to write in this dialogic sense allows students an active role in their learning process:

> If we think of learning as a social process, the process of socially justifying belief, then to teach expository writing . . . involves demonstrating to students that they know something only when they can explain it in writing to the satisfaction of the community of their knowledgeable peers. (652)

Thinking of writing as a social activity puts writing at the center of any curriculum and especially at the center of a composition curriculum—but writing is not conceived as a one-way message to some distant and unfamiliar audience, but instead as a dialogue with people, face-to-face, displaced into writing and about a topic that will have effects on the students' lives.

Bruffee's Collaborative Pedagogy

As noted earlier, Bruffee understands the goal of collaborative writing groups to be to mirror in the classroom the social arrangements that allow knowledge to be generated and maintained. The classroom should be arranged so that students can work as a group of like-minded peers. Bruffee does this in the writing classroom by asking students to work in small groups and to engage in dialogue about all aspects of writing. Bruffee describes the goals and dialogic nature of these writing groups:

> What students do when working collaboratively on their writing is not write or edit or, least of all, read proof. What they do is converse. They talk about the subject and about the assignment. They talk through the writer's understanding of the subject. They converse about their own relationship and, in general, about relationships, in an academic or intellectual context between students and teachers. Most of all they converse about and as part of writing. (645)

Bruffee understands that dialogue is a necessary part of the process of composing. In fact, citing the work of Lev Vygotsky, Bruffee argues that "social speech" is part of learning and performing any complex task.

Vygotsky studied the development of children and noticed that four- or five-year-old children talk aloud while attempting to solve difficult tasks. Children at this age audibly rehearse procedures as they work. Vygotsky found that if he interfered with the child's speech, the child simply stopped; progress resumed only when the child resumed speaking aloud. Vygotsky called this type of speech "instrumental speech" because it aids in getting something done. Children's instrumental speech is not directed toward others, as has been their speech up to this point in their development. The child's social speech can now be "turned inward" and become an "instrument" in helping the child control the physical environment. In short, Vygotsky argued that children first learn "social speech," talk directed at others in order to affect their behavior—to ask for food, a favorite toy, and so on—then, they use "instrumental speech" (that is, social speech turned inward) in the service of learning to control the physical environment and get things done for themselves. As they mature, this "instrumental speech" seems to decrease; but, as Vygotsky and others claim, it becomes what we later experience as "thought"—that is, social speech turned inward.[3] We converse silently with ourselves in ways similar to those that we first learned in social situations. Social speech, the precursor to effective thought, then becomes an essential step in learning. And, as Bruffee argues, social speech is an essential part of learning to write. The collaborative writing group provides the social context for this dialogue about writing to take place.

With these points in mind, Bruffee encourages dialogue about writing in two ways: "face-to-face" and "displaced into writing" (*Short Course* 4th ed. 137). The predominant way that students in Bruffee's class engage in face-to-face dialogue about writing is by reading their papers aloud. For Bruffee,

reading aloud is an important part of learning to read and write constructively because it instantaneously transforms one sort of thing   (written conversation) into another (face-to-conversation). Reading aloud puts the ball into play. (*Short Course* 4th ed. 149)

Reading aloud has benefits for both the individual writer and the group, and it is an important part of building a sense of community among the students in the class. Individuals benefit by overcoming self-consciousness and anxiety about their writing. The instantaneous response helps individual writers acquire a concrete sense of audience. Reading aloud helps them develop a writer's ear: "A lot of awkward, incoherent, pretentious writing results from only seeing writing on the page instead of hearing it there." Writers learn from hearing what is good, as well as what is bad, in prose written by others as well as themselves. Over time they develop a critical awareness and a stronger sense of form because they "can *hear* relationships" among parts and   ideas of their essays (*Short Course* 4th ed. 150). The benefits to the group are also important. Collaborative learning helps students experience the social nature of the writing activity and understand that learning to write is a social act. It builds community and trust because the students know each other's writing.

Most of the reading aloud occurs on days that essay assign-ments are due. On those days, each student reads his or her paper to the class. In addition, students are encouraged to read their own prose aloud to themselves while they are composing, both so that they learn to "hear" their writing and as prepara-tion for the in-class readings.

Each author should read his or her papers to the class. Bruffee argues that instructors should resist reading student papers anonymously:

Because writing is a social act, . . . reading essays aloud anonymously inhibits collaboration. It makes writing less of a conversational exchange among student peers and instead more of a privileged exhange between [student] and teacher, so it increases dependence rather than diminishing it. Anonymity also discourages [students] from talking with [their] fellow students, so it inhibits trust among peers rather than fostering it. (*Short Course* 4th ed. 152)

Anonymous readings only increase students' fear of exposure and reinforce the very anxiety that the anonymous readings are seemingly designed to alleviate. Only extremely anxious students or those with highly personal material that should not be exposed to the class as a whole should be excused from reading their papers aloud—and only once. Later in the term, as students' critical skills and vocabulary for talking about writing increases, students read fewer papers and spend more time critically analyzing all aspects of the papers, including the ideas presented.

Peer criticism, Bruffee's term for the version of collaborative learning he devised for the composition classroom, involves the successful interaction of three factors: the instructor or tutor, the student, and the assignment. Bruffee has devised a three-phase pedagogy:

Each phase begins with an essay assignment. During the class on the day the assignment is due, students should read their essays aloud in class and exchange them. They should exchange essays with different classmates for each assignment as peer critics so that they get diverse criticism of their work. To give students enough practice describing and evaluating essays, they should exchange papers twice for each essay written. When the peer critiques are completed, the teacher should comment on and grade

> descriptions for accuracy, and comment on and grade
> evaluations for accuracy, thoroughness, helpfulness, and
> tact. (*Short Course* 3rd ed. 142)

The students displace the dialogue about writing into written
discourse. Each of the three phases continues and builds on the
one preceding. In the first phase of peer criticism, students
simply describe the essay by writing a descriptive outline of it.
In the second, they write a descriptive outline and evaluate the
writer's technique. In the third phase, in addition to the
descriptive outline and the evaluative comments, the students
comment on the ideas presented in the essay.

In order to provide a clear understanding of Bruffee's dialogic pedagogy, especially since he is most often cited as the
central figure among social–epistemic theorists and his pedagogy is considered "representative" of that view, I will describe
the activities of each of the three phases of Bruffee's pedagogy.[4]

In the first phase of peer criticism, students are asked to write
descriptive outlines of two other students' essays. The goal of
this activity is to

> help inexperienced writers become more critically aware
> of what they are doing when they write. It is a device that
> can help writers become more conscious of the complex
> mental operations they perform in writing, and especially
> more conscious of relationships among the several parts of
> an essay. (97)

In descriptive outlines, students are asked to write "does" and
"says" statements about each of the essay's paragraphs. *Does*
and *says* statements simply describe the function and content of
paragraphs within essays. Here is an example:

Proposition: Cars may be on the way out as our major means of transportation.

Plan: To support the proposition with two reasons.

Paragraph 1:
   does: Introduces the proposition by describing the present situation.
   says: Use of cars is at a peak, but there are signs of change.

Paragraph 2:
   does: Develops the first reason by citing comparative statistics.
   says: Our oil supply is going, and this is made worse by the way car motors waste gas.

Paragraph 3:
   does: develops the second reason by telling an anecdote.
   says: Cars waste time and human energy. (*Short Course* 3rd ed. 98)

Bruffee's textbook provides an entire chapter on developing descriptive outlines and provides numerous examples of student essays with such outlines. Clearly, a descriptive outline provides students with a method of analyzing their written work so as literally to illustrate how its parts are, or are not yet, related. Notice that the kind of response that Bruffee asks students to provide in descriptive outlines differs in some important ways from the "movies of the mind" that Elbow's students are asked to provide writers. Bruffee's students are not asked to describe the experience of reading the essay but to describe its purpose and content simply and concretely.

In the second phase of peer criticism, students provide a descriptive outline, this time with more detail, and they make some evaluative judgments about the writing technique. Bruffee provides the students with general criteria for evaluating unity, coherence, development, style, and mechanics. The students must explain in writing what the essay's strengths are and what could be improved, without indicating whether they deem the essay "good" or "bad." They are cautioned to use tact, and they must support their generalizations with details from the essay in question. In this phase, they can write about the writing technique but not until the third phase are they to comment on any opinions expressed in the essay.

By this stage in Bruffee's pedagogy, the students have learned that it is possible to discuss written material in two ways: they can write descriptive prose about purpose and content and write explanatory prose about writing technique. In the third phase, the students are asked not only to provide a descriptive outline and the explanation of the strengths and weaknesses of the essay but also to respond to the content and take a position on the author's claim. The authors of the essays are asked to comment on or defend the peer criticisms and to explain in what ways, if any, the exchange of views has helped them improve (173). In addition, the second reader on each paper is asked to evaluate the first reader's peer criticism before the essay, the critiques, and the author's defense are delivered to the instructor for his or her evaluations and a grade.

Part of the instructor's role in peer criticism is, in effect, training peer tutors, so some of the comments need to be directed toward gradually developing appropriate critical vocabulary and ways of writing about language. As Bruffee says:

> Sometimes it may be necessary to tell the peer critics that the views they have expressed are not thoroughly thought out or are based on an inaccurate reading of the essay. Sometimes it may be necessary to agree with the criticism,

and yet tell critics that they have been tactless in expression, have not given enough detail to support their generalization, have emphasized trivial points, or have left out the key points entirely. (148)

The instructor needs to be rigorous in evaluating the peer critics' written critiques. Not only does the practice of peer criticism build the peer critics' skill at providing another writer with useful information, but also, and more importantly, peer criticism develops the rhetorical and critical skills that students need to write about issues and ideas that are the common parlance of postsecondary education. For this reason, the peer's written criticism helps develop most of the higher–order critical skills like evaluation, analysis, and synthesis. In this way, then, the instructor's primary role is to represent "the community of mature writers and readers that [students] are trying to join" (*Short Course* 4th ed. 171).

Undoubtedly, these students immediately confront complex audience situations that are difficult to create in many composition classes where the instructor is often the only concrete audience students have. Bruffee makes students aware of the multiple audiences and purposes that writing peer criticism involves:

> The first audience is yourself. Somehow, you have to tell the truth as you see it. The second audience is the teacher, who will evaluate your written peer review and grade it for its thoroughness, accurace, insight, tact and writing quality.
>
> The third and most important audience is the writer of the essay you are reviewing. As a peer reviewer you have to be tactful, constructive, sympathetic, and firm all at once. You have to avoid alienating your peers. At the

same time, you want your peers to respect you enough to want to write equally careful, helpful reviews of your essays in return. (*Short Course* 4th ed. 172-73)

By asking students to engage dialogically in peer criticism, Bruffee provides them with a concrete audience for academic prose, probably for the only time in their careers as student writers.

From a rhetorical standpoint, this is perhaps one of the most effective designs for collaborative learning in the writing classroom because it involves students in numerous dialogues. It involves, for example, face–to–face dialogues with their peers and dialogue displaced into writing, both with the immediate audience of peer and instructor as well as with larger disciplinary and professional communities represented by the reading and writing about ideas that are significant to the various discourse communities that students already belong to and aspire to join. The rhetorical problems of addressing audiences (in this case multiple audiences) for specific purposes are made very concrete for students in ways that they are not when students are asked to think of the instructor as the audience or to imagine a "general" audience. Students are indeed working in a small–scale discourse community and in ways that give them authentic practice in the kinds of social situations that they will encounter when they enter discourse communities beyond the educational system.

However, it is necessary to look more closely at the assumptions and goals of this form of dialogic pedagogy. As I hope I have demonstrated, all dialogic pedagogies are not the same, the underlying assumptions often determining the overall goals and manifestations of the dialogue. Below I discuss some important ways that collaborative learning fails to accomplish those goals.

Community, Conversation, and the
Problem of Authority

The goal of collaborative learning is for students to join the larger community of educated people by engaging in dialogue with and especially *in the manner of* that larger community. The instructor's role is to act as fostering representative of the larger community and to assist students' negotiation of "the rocks and shoals of social relations that may interfere with their getting on with their work together" ("Collaborative Learning" 644–45). According to Bruffee, collaborative learning provides "a particular kind of social context for conversation, a particular kind of community—a community of *status equals: peers*" (642; emphasis added). LeFevre claims that the practical implications for teaching invention and writing itself from a social view lie beyond the classroom as well: "Learning to invent in communities will do more than enable success in classrooms or careers. It is absolutely essential to achieving peace and, indeed, maintaining life on this planet in the twentieth century and beyond" (129). Gregory Clark, in another monograph that explores writing as a social practice, directly links the maintenance of democracy with dialogic pedagogy:

> To say that the texts we write function in interaction with other texts to sustain a process of discursive exchange that resembles conversation, and to say that the function of this conversational exchange is to define and refine the shared knowledge that allows us to act cooperatively within a community, is to assert that the people who participate in that process are political equals who collaborate through their writing in the ongoing project

of self-government. In other words, to adopt this model
of the social function of writing is to adopt a political
vision that is fundamentally democratic.... An education
that sustains collaboration in a community will nurture in
its citizens the skills and the judgment that enable them to
participate constructively in these political conversations,
skills and judgment they develop through the practice of
rhetoric. That is why rhetoric must be placed at the center
of a democratic education. (63)

Unlike the expressivist view that encourages students to see
their power as personal and manifest in personal expression, or
traditional representational models of teaching in which power
is located in the expertise of the instructor, collaborative
learning claims to redistribute power to the community that
students form in the classroom. Students are encouraged to see
themselves as partners in a community's efforts to create and
maintain knowledge and to use dialogue to negotiate entrance
into new discourse communities. Collaborative learning theorists assume that students' voices will become part of ongoing
and significant dialogues; they will come to see themselves as
participating in the conversation of humankind.

However, many collaborative learning advocates naively
believe that democratic exchange and concomitant student
empowerment are obvious by-products of dialogue within the
group. As several critics argue, asking students to collaborate
does not necessarily lead to the kind of social situations where
truly democratic dialogue can take place. Despite the ascen-
dancy of social constructionism in composition studies, several
scholars recently have provided important critiques of social
construction in the field.

Gere, for example, acknowledges the differences in power
relationships in self-sponsored groups and in institutionally-

sponsored groups. Self-sponsored writing groups (Elbow's teacherless class is a good example) come together out of "natural affinity," such as occupation, status, or other shared concerns (50). Often this initial affinity is enough to foster goodwill and mutual respect among members. In this positive atmosphere, members are more likely to submit their writing to the scrutiny and criticism of the group. Gere sees these groups as sharing authority more easily and, thus, as inherently more democratic. She writes:

> In surrendering their writing, group members simultaneously give and accept authority. They give other individuals the right to express reactions and make suggestions and with that giving of authority goes the implicit willingness to credit (at least in part) the responses of their peers with authority. (50)

In self-sponsored writing groups, authority is only temporarily and contingently given to the other members of the group. Individual members always "retain the right to leave the group, or to disregard the comments or advice of others" (50).

In contrast, in school-sponsored writing groups the instructor maintains authority and the students may or may not have any shared affinities. In most postsecondary composition classes, instructors structure the tasks, evaluate performance, and assign grades. The uneven power relationship between the instructor and the students in school-sponsored writing groups makes it more difficult to orchestrate the necessary kinds of social situations that will allow students to engage in meaningful dialogue.[5] By "meaningful," I mean that students are not just unthinkingly performing tasks that the instructor has set but are actively and critically involved. It is likely that students may be more worried about performing to instructor expectations than about engaging in substantive dialogue with their peers. If the emphasis remains on fulfilling the dictates of the instructor, students do not, even in collaborative learning situations, become independent thinkers. In this event, collaborative learning offers no inherently better options for learning than more traditional "teacher–centered" methods.

It is exactly the potential for and actual fact of uneven power relationships among group members that has most worried critics of collaborative teaching methods. Thomas S. Johnson is concerned that collaborative learning groups can produce "Orwellian 'groupthink'" and has dubbed Bruffee's method of peer criticism: "peer indoctrination classes" (76). Pedro Beade worries that Bruffee's methods, if carried to the extreme, could be used to justify "a crazy, totalitarian state" (708). Donald C. Stewart has expressed similar concerns. These fears may seem somewhat extreme, but, in fact, as several critics have convincingly argued, matters of difference among students, like class and gender, do produce uneven power relationships that authorize some members' voices and tend to silence or ignore others', making it difficult for all group members to engage in status–equal dialogue. As Evelyn Ashton–Jones points out, there is the assumption among writing group theorists

> that those speaking from marginalized and "different" perspectives—be it from the perspective of race, ethnicity, gender, class, age, sexual orientation, or occupation—will, in fact, have access to the conversation and, further, that the dynamics of the conversation itself will remain unaffected by a given participant's "difference." (3)

It is naive to think that the power imbalances evident in social relationships outside the classroom—imbalances based on gender, race, and class, for instance—can be nullified inside the classroom. And as Greg Myers argues, it is factors such as class, ethnicity, and race that often determine who will be enrolled and, therefore, who can participate in the dialogue in the first place (167). It is not reasonable to assume that students in school–sponsored writing groups will be immune to the influence of these uneven power relationships and, therefore, that they can engage in dialogue with each other on an equal footing. If, in fact, all students are not considered to be equal members of the community, then the assumptions of and claims for a collaborative pedagogy based on social–epistemic theories of knowledge belie the actuality of the social situations in which students and instructors exist.

Unfortunately, the uneven power relationships that affect the social context of composition classrooms often are "invisible" because they reproduce in our actions and speech the socially inscribed and largely unexamined assumptions and stereotypes that comprise social relations in society at large, even though educators often desire, with the best intentions, to view their classrooms as "neutral spaces" or "level playing fields" where all students receive an equal chance to learn. Gender is one such factor that often affects our interpersonal relationships in such "invisible" ways.

Ashton–Jones, in a compelling feminist critique, points out the gender blindness in writing group theory, including the feminist theories that welcome collaborative learning as compatible with feminism (5-6). Feminism's almost wholesale adoption of collaborative learning, she argues, "does not acknowledge the role that gender may play in group dynamics" (10). She cites numerous sociolinguistic studies of conversational groups to demonstrate her concerns. From these studies it is clear that women and men do not operate on equal terms in conversational situations. For instance, women are more likely to assume responsibility for maintaining the dialogue and, yet, have fewer opportunities to initiate conversations that are sustained by their male counterparts. Men interrupted or overlapped in conversational situations from seventy-five to ninety-six percent of the time when the conversation was among mixed-sex conversants. As Ashton-Jones elaborates:

> The conversational difficulty male interruptions and overlaps cause are underscored by the response they elicit from women: silence . . . suggest[ing] not only that being interrupted or overlapped or not receiving attentive reinforcement elicits immediate silence, but that these speech events may elicit silence in women *overall*. (17)

These studies and the others that Ashton-Jones cites indicate the difficulty women face in attempting to maintain an "equal footing" with their male conversants. I would agree with the conclusion that Ashton-Jones draws from these studies of gender dynamics in conversation:

> The conversational events that these studies describe are not likely to magically disappear when the scene of meaning-making shifts to collaborative learning groups. On the contrary, it is more likely that in writing groups women and men's behavior will parallel the conversational events described in these studies, men interacting as individualists pressing to get across and win their points of view—thus controlling the realities produced in these writing communities—and women shouldering the major share of the necessary interactional work. (21)

Clearly, it cannot be assumed that dialogic groups that composition instructors attempt to form will actually engage *all* students equally in learning. As Ashton-Jones so aptly puts it, "The students who engage in such conversations cannot be conflated under the rubric of *student*; as women and men, they are gender–differentiated and, consequently, status–differentiated" (30).

All students enter composition classrooms as "status–differentiated." Collaborative learning theory, at least from a social-epistemic perspective, has not yet provided an adequate description of how these differences and the inevitable resulting conflicts are to be dealt with democratically. One reason so little attention is paid to student differences is that collaborative learning theorists assume that those differences will be engaged as students unquestioningly accept the norms, values, and view of reality of the larger group.

Myers, concerned about the dangers of "harnessing peer influence," reminds us, "Any teacher who uses group discussions or projects has seen that they can, on occasion, be fierce enforcers of conformity" (159). He argues that both instructor and students bring to the classroom an "ideology" that reproduces itself in their social interactions. Myers uses the term *ideology*, not in the sense of "false ideology" as in early Marxism, but as "the whole systems of thought and belief that goes with a social and economic system, the thoughts that structure our thinking so deeply that we take them for granted, as the nature of the real world" (156). One reproduces these belief structures by a process of adopting and sustaining them, often without evaluating them. With these concepts in mind, Myers argues that while Bruffee shows us that belief structures—the ways we construe reality—"can be seen as a social construct, he does not give us any way to criticize this construct" (166). Myers elaborates, "Having discovered the role of consensus in the production of knowledge, [Bruffee] takes this consensus as something that just is, rather than as something that might be good or bad" (166). Along with Myers, I question collaborative learning's ability to introduce students to new discourse communities. It seems just as likely that collaborative learning will confine them to unquestioned, unexamined ideological structures.

Along these same lines, I would argue that Bruffee and other social constructionists place too much emphasis on students' making themselves into socially acceptable initiates; in collaborative methods, learning is viewed as a process of "reacculturation." In Bruffee's pedagogy, the process of negotiating entry into new knowledge communities is largely seen as a one-way process in which the students must accomplish a great deal of accommodation to the larger group. The larger group is the "inside," and the students appear in Bruffee's rhetoric as "outside," seeming to speak an unfamiliar language and clamoring to get in. The students' principal task is to adapt to and accept the values and norms of the knowledge communities that they intend to join. They do this by imitating the dialogue of those who are already members—not by questioning the content of the dialogue or the values and norms of the established community.

In the next chapter, I will examine the dialogic pedagogical theories of Paulo Freire and other liberatory learning theorists and consider how these theories have been adapted in postsecondary composition. Radical pedagogy, as it is sometimes called, encompasses a social view of knowledge and of communication that is centrally concerned with dialogue, not only among status–equal peers but also among oppressed groups and the social institutions that oppress them. The goal of this pedagogy is for students to engage oppressive social structures critically in a dialogue that leads to transformation of those structures. Radical pedagogy extends the collaborative view to include a strong liberatory component in which dialogue is even more central to the success of the goals of the pedagogy and which may offer hope of dealing with some of the problems that collaborative learning is unable to resolve.

Notes

1. See Mason, James, and Abercrombie.

2. Students are *re*acculturated in the sense that they arrive in the classroom as members of some discourse communities and through collaborative work join others.

3. Of course, Vygotsky never claims that mature thought is equivalent to social speech. Thought is condensed, one word or group of words often standing in for whole complexes of ideas. Vygotsky argues that writing is thought made social again. There is much discussion in composition studies as to the nature of the relationship of thought and writing.

4. Bruffee asks students to write five-hundred word, three-paragraph essays in which the proposition is stated in the last sentence of the first paragraph and the two following paragraphs support the proposition. The later writing tasks allow students to add a fourth, concluding paragraph. He justifies this on several grounds: (a) it provides the students with a form that is adaptable to many situations; (b) it provides the instructor (and the students) with consistency in organizational patterns in the student essays, thereby allowing them both more focus on matters of rhetoric and content. The wisdom of this practice is

doubtful; however, a discussion of the problems of this aspect of his pedagogy is tangential to the discussion of dialogue. Also, please assume that the students have done some classroom practice in the kinds of activities that they will be asked to perform on their own in the peer criticisms. (*Short Course* 3rd ed. 20–27, passim)

5. Of course, there is always the potential that a hierarchy will develop even in self-sponsored writing groups, but these groups have the authority to take back power or to disband if some individuals become oppressive. Students in institutionally-sponsored writing groups rarely have that option.

Dialogism and Radical Pedagogy

Tell me, and I'll forget. Show me, and I may not remember. Involve me, and I'll understand.
—Native American Saying

Perhaps in no other area of composition studies and literacy training is dialogism more central than in the approach most often called "liberatory learning." Liberatory learning, or radical pedagogy, was developed primarily by Third World literacy educators such as Ivan Illich and Paulo Freire. Concerned with the masses of poor and uneducated people in rapidly developing countries who are able to be exploited precisely because of their illiteracy, liberatory learning specialists have developed pedagogies for teaching reading and writing to these people so as to give them the critical tools necessary to help prevent themselves from remaining "oppressed."

The radical pedagogy of Brazilian educator Paulo Freire is the most well known to compositionists. In fact, Freirean theory and pedagogy have become central to much recent work in composition. Freire's pedagogy is entirely based on dialogic methods that attempt to subvert the traditional form of education as a "depositing" of information in students. He attempts to erect in its place a form of instruction that allows students to become full participants in their own education. Recently, composition specialists have adapted these approaches to college-level writing instruction in the U.S.

Before discussing the role of dialogism in Freire's pedagogy, it is necessary to examine the general goals of liberatory learning and its attempt to serve as an alternative to traditional educational forms. It is also necessary to discuss Freire's concept of praxis and his rejection of the Cartesian subject/object dichotomy.

Liberatory Learning and Critical Consciousness

Freire proposes liberatory learning as a way to counter the traditional model of education, what he calls the "banking" or "nutritionist" model. In this traditional view, the teacher possesses objective knowledge and transmits it to receptive students—metaphorically deposits it, as in making a bank deposit. According to Freire, this model turns students into

> "containers," into "receptacles" to be filled by the teacher. The more completely he fills the receptacles, the better teacher he is. The more meekly the receptacles permit themselves to be filled, the better students they are. (*Oppressed* 58)

The teacher is the "narrator" of the knowledge and the students' task is to learn the "narrated content" and repeat it back unchanged.

Freire claims that this model of education reflects the "attitudes and practices" of an "oppressive society as a whole." He lists in detail the characteristics of "banking education":

a. the teacher teaches and the students are taught;
b. the teacher knows everything and the students know nothing;
c. the teacher thinks and the students are thought about;

d. the teacher talks and the students listen—meekly;

e. the teacher disciplines and the students are disciplined;

f. the teacher chooses and enforces his choice, and the students comply;

g. the teacher acts and the students have the illusion of acting through the action of the teacher;

h. the teacher chooses the program content, and the students (who were not consulted) adapt to it;

i. the teacher confuses the authority of knowledge with his own professional authority, which he sets in opposition to the freedom of the students;

j. the teacher is the subject of the learning process, while the pupils are mere objects. (*Oppressed* 59)

In this model, the teacher possesses all authority; the students have none. The world is perceived as a static place and therefore knowledge of it is also static and unchanging. Knowledge becomes something that can be ingested whole and without any critical reflection. In addition, this kind of education maintains people as objects, not as people able to take action in the world.

For Freire, humans differ from animals precisely in their ability to reflect on their lives and to take action to transform the material world around them. Humanity is reflective and active within the materiality of the concrete, historical world (87). Yet, many people never develop as subjects or agents because of their social position; the ability to think critically and to take action in the world is unimaginable to such people: they become the oppressed, the dehumanized, the illiterate. Freire defines the struggle to gain back one's stolen humanity as "man's vocation":[1]

While both humanization and dehumanization are real alternatives, only the first is man's vocation. This vocation is constantly negated, yet it is affirmed by that very negation. It is thwarted by injustice, exploitation, oppression, and the violence of the oppressors; it is affirmed by the yearning of the oppressed for freedom and justice, and by their struggle to recover their lost humanity. (*Oppressed* 28)

Dehumanization, or seeing groups of people as objects rather than subjects, is the hallmark of oppression and is further maintained by the "banking" model of education. Based on a dialogic methodology, liberatory learning is the process by which the oppressed begin the struggle for the humanity that has been wrested from them by the oppressors.

In this struggle, students begin to see themselves as "subjects," as people with power, rather than as objects that simply work or perform at the will of others. The subject position that they gain involves the transformation of the concrete, historical limit situations that characterize their oppression. The task of liberatory learning is to present the "limit situation" as an intellectual problem to be solved by the learner (*Oppressed* 89). In other words, learners must first understand the limits placed on them by the oppressive situation they find themselves in; then, rather than see this situation as hopeless, they must learn to see it as a challenge. That is, through a problem–solving process they must gain hope and the will to transform their oppressive life situations. Finally, they must take action and thereby bring about change *for themselves*. They become thinkers and actors, true agents, whereas before they saw their oppressors as the only people who could legitimately think and act.

Freire stresses two important points repeatedly. First, the oppressed must free themselves. The dominant class cannot bestow freedom or knowledge on the masses as a gift; this only

results in false generosity and does not allow people to overcome dependency. The dominant classes will not free the
oppressed whom they depend upon for their privilege, and
since the oppressors perceive the dominated as less than human, they will not give the oppressed truly what they need to
become fully human and fully free from domination.[2]

Neither can the dominant class establish schools that bestow
knowledge on the oppressed if the content of the curriculum is
determined solely by the dominant group. Such a curriculum
will not mean anything to the oppressed, as it reflects the values
and privilege of the dominant group. In this way, schools
function as tools of domination that only transform the oppressed (those that stay in the system) into oppressors. As
Freire writes:

> As alienated men, they cannot overcome their dependency
> by "incorporation" into the very structure responsible for
> their dependency. There is no other road to
> humanization—theirs as well as everyone else's—but
> authentic transformation of the dehumanizing structure.
> (*Cultural Action* 11)

Liberation does not occur without transformation of the social
structure, which includes the social structure of schooling, as
well as the consciousness of the people.

The banking model of education reinforces the reality
named by the oppressor. In contrast, the task of liberatory
learning is for the oppressed to emerge from this reality into
one that they name for themselves. Freire writes:

> One of the gravest obstacles to the achievement of liberation
> is that oppressive reality absorbs those within it and
> thereby acts to submerge men's consciousness.

Functionally, oppression is domesticating. To no longer
be prey to its force, one must emerge from it and turn
upon it. This can only be done by means of the praxis:
reflection and action upon the world in order to transform
it. (*Oppressed* 36)

It is this process of emerging from a dominant reality that
allows people to engage in the continuing process of what
Freire calls *conscientização*: political and personal consciousness.
One gains this kind of critical consciousness through *praxis*—
that is, by reflecting and acting upon the world dialogically
with others in order to transform it.

Basic to Freire's theory is rejection of the Cartesian subject/
object dichotomy. Freire emphasizes the necessity of perceiv-
ing subject/object as a unity that can only be understood in a
dialectical relationship if praxis is to be effective:

To deny the importance of subjectivity in the process of
transforming the world and history is naive and simplistic.
It is to admit the impossible: a world without men. This
objectivist position is as ingenuous as that of subjectivism,
which postulates men without a world. World and men
do not exist apart from each other, they exist in constant
interaction. (*Oppressed* 35–36)

In the *Politics of Education*, he elaborates on the importance of
the relationship between the subject/object dialectic and the
concept of praxis. Praxis is the unity of reflection and action
and can only be conceived when one leaves behind the subject/
object duality. In other words, if we accept the subjectivist view
of the world and believe that changing consciousness will lead
to social change, we are naive because the concrete social
structures of oppressive society remain intact. To illustrate,

Freire provides this example: "The possibilities that I had for transcending the narrow limits of a five-by-two-foot cell in which I was locked after the April 1964 Brazilian *coup d'etat*, were not sufficient to change my condition as prisoner" (154).

On the other hand, the objectivist view of changing the concrete conditions alone, mere activism, leaves people without the will or "know-how" to continue to operate as fully human and liberated beings. Changing the material conditions alone does nothing to change the perceptions created with the establishment of domination. If our perceptions are informed solely by one side of the subject/object duality, praxis ceases to function. True praxis must involve reflection and action in a unity (*Politics of Education* 154–55).

In short, Freire's pedagogy is an attempt to break down the traditional educational hierarchy so as to enable students to become full participants in the educational process. As "subjects" students learn to act in the world on their own behalf. Once students gain this agency, they have come a long way in freeing themselves from the type of oppressive situation Freire describes. Students accomplish this empowerment through a thoroughly dialogic pedagogy.

Freirean Dialogics

As Freire explains, in the banking model teachers and students occupy opposing poles:

The teacher presents himself to his students as their necessary opposite; by considering their ignorance absolute, he justifies his own existence. The students . . . accept their ignorance as justifying the teacher's existence. . . . They never discover that they educate the teacher. (*Oppressed* 58–59)

Liberatory learning attempts to reconcile these poles so that both participants are "simultaneously teachers *and* students" (59). This reconciliation takes place in dialogue between new positions that necessarily include each other: "teacher–student with students–teachers" (67). The teacher and student must develop a way of acting that involves communication, or dialogue, rather than the teacher making knowledge deposits that the student accepts unquestioningly. Freire writes:

> The important thing, from the point of view of libertarian education, is for men to come to feel like masters of their thinking by discussing the thinking and views of the world explicitly or implicitly manifest in their own suggestions and those of their comrades. (*Oppressed* 118)

Not only is the classroom conceived as a site of dialogue, but the curricular content is also developed in dialogue with the students:

> Because this view of education starts with the conviction that it cannot present its own program but *must search for this program dialogically with the people,* it serves to introduce the pedagogy of the oppressed, in the elaboration of which *the oppressed must participate.* (*Oppressed* 118; emphasis added)

More importantly, dialogue is the situation in which praxis— reflection plus action in Freire's system—takes place. Both the content of the curriculum and the way the curriculum is dealt with are dialogical.

In developing the curriculum in Third World settings, progressive educators live among the illiterate peasants for a time "in order to come to know through dialogue with them both their *objective situation* and their *awareness* of that situation" (84). During this process, they meet in groups with the residents and discuss what they see and hear, listening again to the residents as a check against their perceptions. The educators develop these common perceptions into *generative themes* to be presented back to the students in the educational program.[3] Then the group begins to assemble codifications (pictures or drawings in the preliterate stage, passages to read in the postliterate stage) based on the generative themes, which *re-present* to students their reality as it has been jointly grasped in the dialogic groups of co-investigators. After the presentation of the codifications to a group of students who decode them, the group meets again, adjusts the material, and expands it as new and peripheral themes emerge from the dialogue.

Equally important, the educators must understand how the residents view their situation, because the dialogue requires that the residents and the educators become increasingly conscious of their emerging consciousness. This becoming aware of one's own consciousness is essential to the emergence of the oppressed from oppression. As Freire explains:

In the process of decoding [the codifications], the participants externalize their thematics and thereby make explicit their "real consciousness" of the world. As they do this, they themselves begin to see how they acted while actually experiencing the situation they are now analyzing, and thus reach a "perception of their previous perception." By achieving this awareness, they come to perceive reality differently.... By stimulating "perception of the previous perception" and "knowledge of the previous knowledge," decoding stimulates the appearance of a new perception and the development of new knowledge. (*Oppressed* 108)

100 *Literacy, Ideology, Dialogue*

The students are presented with codifications that produce contradictions: what I perceive today versus when the experience depicted in the codification happened; what I perceive versus what you perceive; and so on. Through the perception of these contradictions in dialogue with others, the students objectify their perceptions of the world; their very perception becomes problematic. They must deal with the fact that perception is changeable—a fact hidden from students when they are presented with static, prepackaged knowledge as in the banking model of education:

> Whereas the banking method directly or indirectly reinforces men's fatalistic perception of their situation, the problem-posing method presents this very situation to them as a problem. As the situation becomes the object of their cognition, the naive or magical perception which produced their fatalism gives way to perception which is able to perceive itself even as it perceived reality, and can thus be critically objective about that reality. (73)

Dialogue is important because the students' reflection does not take place in the abstract but always in the context of the world as they are coming to understand it in dialogue *with others* as they too are coming to understand it.

Thus, this dialogic is not Socratic, because it rejects a view of knowledge and truth as transcendent and affirms an interactional, constructionist view:

> Socratic intellectualism—which mistook the definition of the concept for knowledge of the thing defined and this knowledge as virtue—did not constitute a true pedagogy of knowing, even though it was dialogical. . . . For Plato the *prise de conscience* did not refer to what man knew or

did not know or knew badly about his dialectical relationship with the world; it was concerned rather with what man once knew and forgot at birth. To know was to remember or recollect forgotten knowledge. (*Politics* 55)

In Freirean dialogic there is no higher plain of perfect forms to rediscover. The dialogue is always about the dialectic of people and the concrete world, the dialectic of subject and object.

In sum, dialogue breaks down the banking model of education, replacing it with the joint effort of student and instructor in mutual intellectual inquiry. Through this cooperation, both student and instructor learn and teach; both are actively engaged in an investigation of life and perception. The social structure of the traditional classroom is broken down, and the classroom becomes an enactment of democracy. The students become like the citizens of a democracy: active in the processes that affect their lives. What is important about this kind of dialogue is its subversion of hierarchy; only in a dialogic relation between equals can the oppressed begin to express the reality of their lives, not as defined by the oppressor but as the oppressed experience it. Freire writes:

Dialogue cannot be reduced to the act of one person's "depositing" ideas in another, nor can it become a simple exchange of ideas to be "consumed" by the discussants. Nor yet is it a hostile, polemical argument between men who are committed neither to the naming of the world, nor the search for truth, but rather to the imposition of their own truth. Because dialogue is an encounter among men who name the world, it must not be a situation where some men name on behalf of others. (*Oppressed* 77)

This kind of liberatory and democratic dialogue is often difficult to achieve, and Freire warns that there are six necessary conditions for dialogue to be effective and not to become another form of domination: love, humility, faith in humanity, trust, hope, and, critical thinking. The dialogue must be "critical" leading to critical consciousness because only then can the oppressive, dehumanizing social situations that envelop us be perceived as challenges to be met and transformed.

Importing Freirean Theory into Composition

Much of Freire's writing avoids concrete examples or explicit descriptions because he wants to circumvent the wholesale transference of methods to contexts outside those that they were specifically devised for; the methods designed for illiterate peasants in Brazil, for example, are not necessarily meant to work with other populations. Freire stresses repeatedly that the theoretical framework transfers but the actual methods must grow from the dialogic investigation with the students of their own environment and perceptions. Nevertheless, many compositionists have attempted to methodologize Freire's work. Because liberatory learning is conceived explicitly for the purpose of teaching literacy, many in composition studies have found its theoretical framework inspiring and have tried to apply it to college-level composition classrooms.

Ira Shor is one of the first teachers in the U.S. to attempt to apply Freirean theory to college-level composition classes. His various articles and books on and coauthored with Freire have established him as one of the foremost Freireans in the U.S. In fact, Shor has become so closely associated with Freire and his pedagogy that no one in composition studies has bothered to examine Shor's work critically to determine if his pedagogical approach is in any way Freirean. His *Critical Teaching and Everyday Life* first appeared in 1980 and has been reprinted several times; it continues to influence compositionists interested in the theory of liberatory pedagogy. Chapter four of Shor's book, "Monday Morning: Critical Literacy and the Theme of 'Work,'" describes a class that Shor designed around the theme of work. Shor developed and refined his applications of Freire while working with working–class students during the period of open admissions in the City University of New York (1971–1977), which, Shor says, "de–stabilized New York's public academy long enough for experiments in liberatory teaching" (127).

He justifies using a theoretical frame developed for preliterate peasants in the Third World this way:

> Domination by mass culture, in an advanced society like the U.S., has left the population either functionally illiterate or uncritically literate, and politically undeveloped. The need for conscientization exists, to counter the interferences to critical thought in daily life. The questions of dialogic pedagogy, cultural democracy, critical awareness and structural perception are urgently relevant in this technically advanced culture. (127)

North American students are somewhat like Freire's oppressed peasants: they have been educated largely in the "banking" paradigm that, as noted earlier, maintains students in the passive role of listener, rarely giving them the opportunity to engage actively as agents in their education. They become habituated to passivity by a host of educational practices that more often than not privilege conformity and an unquestioning acceptance of authority. The ones who make it to postsecondary education are the ones who learned to play the game of schooling—which doesn't necessarily reward curiosity and inquiry as much as memorization of facts and procedures.

Shor's method is designed to overcome students' alienation, which he sees as their "largest learning problem." The students' development is rapid once the presence of the teacher "withers away," and they begin to emerge as "subjects of the learning process" (103). Like Freire's approach utilizing generative themes and codifications, Shor's strategy is to help students "re-experience" the ordinary:

> Single features of everyday life are isolated as themes for study. This is the method which uproots the ordinary pieces of experience for extra-ordinary reflection. A critical dialogue around an abstracted part of life permits students to gain detachment from the structure of social relations inside and outside their minds. (99)

Shor has developed courses around several "pieces of experience"—for example, the theme of work. However, he has also organized courses around such themes as hamburgers, sex and gender relations, and utopia. Shor's course focusing on the theme of work reveals how Freirean theory can be misused and how a true dialogic approach can be undermined even in the name of dialogic pedagogy.

The early stages of Shor's course on work are designed to accomplish two objectives: first, to give students some "take-away literacy modes" that they can employ later without teachers; and second, to wean them away from their reliance on the authority of the teacher while fostering their development as subjects by building on the skills they already have.

Shor shows students two simple strategies: prewriting and dictation. Shor presents prewriting as three easy steps: think, itemize, write. For their first in-class assignment, "The worst teacher I ever had," he asks students to visualize what they want to write about, then to list what they see, and finally to compose "a good-sized paragraph" (130).

The dictation exercise is meant to help students build on their speaking skills. One student dictates while another records verbatim what is said; they then change places. Again, they employ the prewriting strategy first. According to Shor, this method accomplishes several things:

> This is a style of writing which encourages peer relations. The students have to cooperate to get the work done; the teacher does not monitor them. They need to listen carefully to each other, something they are conditioned against through the teacher–centered schooling in their pasts. . . . In their native idiom, students have strong speaking skills, so it is a great resource to have composition evolve from their verbal talent. (131)

Thus, according to Shor, the students begin to make connections between the oral language skills they already have and the written language skill they are trying to acquire. In addition, both these modes encourage the students' independence from the teacher.

But Shor also wants to begin to develop students' ability to think abstractly. After the students have completed the "worst teacher" compositions, he then poses the more general question: "What is a bad teacher?" From the specific detail of the students' essays, Shor records as the students compile a list of the attributes of a bad teacher. According to Shor, "This involves the simple philosophical operation of abstracting a general case from specific details; it's a foundation for structural perception, and a logical base for categorical understanding" (132). In this way, the students gain a higher degree of literacy and critical thinking skills simultaneously, drawing on the simple examination of their ordinary experiences with teachers.

The next writing assignment begins the examination of another ordinary aspect of student lives and introduces the examination of the course's generative theme: work. The students are asked to write on "The Worst Job I Ever Had," and they follow the same procedure just described. After the students have composed their essays using the prewriting technique, Shor introduces a technique he calls *voicing*: "a self-editing tool which calls on students to use the natural grammar in their speaking voices." The students read their writing aloud; Shor tells them that whenever they stumble or hesitate, "your strong speaking skills are being interfered with by your less developed writing skills" (133). Of course, often one's speaking skills are so much more developed that they will not even acknowledge what the eye is actually seeing on the page. To remedy this problem, Shor has the students "voice" in pairs. One student reads aloud over the shoulder of another who reads silently and stops the speaker "whenever the speaker passes over something that the reader notices" (135). Over time, the speaker's eye catches up with the strong speaking voice, and the students acquire another "take-away" literacy skill. And again, this exercise enhances peer relations; it takes emphasis away from the teacher and focuses students' attention on their own and each other's writing (135).[4]

After students have worked several sessions on voicing technique, Shor asks for two volunteers to share their essays: "As they read, the saga of bad work experiences stirs a lot of interest. Students spontaneously engage in dialogue about jobs they have held in common. Just about everyone has something to offer to the conversation" (136). The students then construct two lists, one of those things the two students' worst job had "in common," and another of things "not in common." Shor acts merely as recorder; the concepts grow from the students' dialogue. This activity begins the critical reflection on the ordinary subject of work. As Shor often reminds his readers, the students furnish the data for the inquiry, and because it is directly related to their concrete experience, they have a stake in the inquiry—the classroom is no longer so alienating: "The mind practices re-perceiving reality into meaningful shapes" (137).

At this point in the sequence, Shor asks the students to examine the two lists for contradictions and validity. The students sometimes request that the student essays be reread; items are sometimes deleted and new ones added; sometimes the students find they must solicit more information from the student authors. Shor then asks an even more abstract question: "What are all the aspects of a job?" (137). Clearly, he provides students with a strategy for generalizing about and analyzing any subject.

At first, the critical thinking and the literacy skills seem to be developing on separate but parallel tracks, but as Shor explains,

> Most of my students have never looked this closely at their jobs, their writings, each other, or the teacher. The careful attention to detail is what their English teachers have lectured to them under the rubrics of "paragraph development" and "theme organization." Studied as a rhetorical lesson instead of a lesson in critically re-perceiving reality, "paragraph development" has of course not developed inside my students. By preparing composite lists, we construct a systematic breakdown of a discrete corner of life. (137)

Thus, the students are taught a strategy for discovering the details necessary for "good paragraph development." Shor continues to develop deeper and deeper thinking skills while the students continue to write and learn more literacy skills. They move on to a discussion of union labor as a kind of working condition, then on to readings, where Shor teaches take–away reading skills. The students' final assignment is to write two profiles of two different working people.

The Reflection and Action Dialectic Ignored

While Shor is quite clear about the growth of writing and thinking skills in his students, he is rather vague about their ability to fulfill the action side of Freire's dialectic between reflection and action. These students never move into any larger dialogue outside the classroom. The dialogue remains between Shor and his students; it is limited and self–contained. This dialogue is valuable in concept building but lacks the radical revolutionary nature that Freire stresses in the theory he developed. Like collaborative learning, this kind of dialogue does not necessarily lead to liberation and can just as easily serve indoctrination and the reproduction of dominant ideology.[5]

Shor mentions, almost in an aside, that "students who practice these conceptual exercises have been transforming themselves into people who can observe carefully and who can generalize but they do not yet have a commitment to transform what they have abstracted" (138). Freire is clear both in his early and later writings that any method that does not include the dialectic between reflection and action is not liberatory but remains, like the banking method, a means of indoctrination into the dominant class. In that case, no one is liberated, no social transformation is achieved, the hierarchy of oppressor and oppressed remains.

At the point in the curriculum when Shor introduces union jobs, he claims that students' commitment to transformation heretofore has been lacking but that some progress toward "transcendent perception can be gained" (138). Yet, it is at this point that Shor seems to take over the curriculum, abandoning the liberatory paradigm and adopting the banking method. He claims that his students' knowledge of trade unionism is "uneven and unclear," that information about benefits such as "fixed hourly rates plus periodic increments, sick pay, overtime, paid vacations and pensions plans," and a history of trade unionism is "integrated here rather organically" (138-39). Since Shor does not provide a clear description of the sources he supplies for this section as he does for other assignments, and since he makes it clear that the students cannot furnish that data from their own experience, we can assume that he "integrates" this information via lectures. Lecturing in itself is not necessarily bad, but as Shor himself writes in the theoretical chapter preceding this course description,

> the crux of liberatory theory rests in the empowering animation of critical consciousness, through the students' object–subject switch, in an egalitarian, experience–based dialogue, initiated by a teacher functioning in a mobile complex of roles. (122-23)

The experience–based dialogue is clearly abandoned by Shor when he introduces this section of the curriculum content. It seems that Shor has moved away from his students' "everyday lives" and on to his own academic interests. He has flipped the students back into the object position and placed himself firmly in the subject position of expert. Moreover, he makes this reversion at exactly the time when he claims that students should be emerging from the object position. At one point, Shor actually says that "questions about labor suggest themselves" (139). Undoubtedly, Shor is the only one to suggest any questions that are taken seriously as part of the curriculum.

What a liberatory theorist would expect to see happening at this point is the students beginning to raise questions, to direct the classroom inquiry themselves and, more importantly, to address the concrete conditions under which they work as problems that call for solutions. Some sort of social dialogue should emerge—a dialogue initiated by the students whose transformed understanding of their position in the work force enables them to envision some possibility for change.

Instead, Shor suggests that the students be asked to "compose a short speech from the point of view of corporate management and from the perspective of the workers, with each explaining in their own idioms why unions are good or bad" (139). These short speeches become merely comparison and contrast exercises, measuring the level of understanding of the concepts that the instructor presents. This is nothing like the transformative reflection and action envisioned in liberatory theory. Shor claims, "The moment when another section of social life—like trade unionism—takes systematic shape in the imagination is a pedagogical time rich in possibilities" (139). Yet, Shor has abandoned the methodology that, as he himself promised, could allow the richest of possibilities: the students' own emergence into independent critical consciousness, or, to use Freire's term, conscientization. Rather than a rich, truly democratic dialogue among students and teacher as equals, Shor's course devolves to one of limited and sometimes one-way communication.

In Shor's classroom, writing never becomes dialogic or "rhetorical"; it is never directed to anyone for any purpose other than to fulfill assignments and to receive a grade. As I have argued before in this study, if students are continually asked to write in arhetorical situations, they never gain the audience-analysis skills that can act as guidelines for estimating the success of any piece of writing that they may produce.

More importantly, they never get to experience how language and action work themselves out in situations outside the classroom where written discourse has effects on people's lives. They never experience their writing as part of a dialogue with an "other." In Shor's methodology, reading and writing remain activities one does *in school*—activities that have little or no use in any other situation in the students' lives (especially in the low-paying, low-level jobs that the students have access to and experience with). One of the reasons that Freire's literacy campaigns have been so successful is that the link between reflection and action is never forgotten. In a matter of months rather than years, Freire is able to bring people from illiteracy to functional literacy. Because these people are expected to apply their new skills to problems that directly affect the quality of their lives, they see how discourse, especially the privileged written kind, functions in their relationships with the oppressive social situations that envelop them. The dialogue with the teacher and classmates moves on to a transforming dialogue with the world. However, with Shor's method, dialogue is limited to the classroom and to subjects introduced by and of primary interest to the teacher. Shor's students talk to Shor and not to their community. Since students are never moved to take any action to improve their own working conditions, their writing never becomes truly social or dialogic in a Freirean sense.

Finally, as discussed earlier, another basic tenet of Freirean theory is that the content of the curriculum be developed in dialogue with the community of students. Only in the process of *dialogic* inquiry with the students can the educator gain an understanding of the concrete situation in which the students live and how they perceive that situation. This dialogic inquiry starts before classes are actually formed and continues during the formal schooling. What is striking about Shor's choice of theme—work—is that it so nearly matches his own interests in Marxist analysis.[6] In addition, this does not represent a two-way, dialogic process. Shor poses the questions that the students then answer. Not one student question ever emerges to become part of the curriculum. Although Freire did not envisione a situation in which the educator is *never* allowed to pose questions or to decide what the content will be, he is clear nonetheless that unless the basic direction of the inquiry grows out of a dialogue with the students, liberation is unlikely and indoctrination inevitable. Shor's topic of work and unionism is imposed without consultation with the students. Gail Stygall questions Shor's imposition of the theme of work on his students:

> Perhaps Shor's female students would have liked to have chosen women's roles as a generative theme. Perhaps his black students would have chosen race. And perhaps his Hispanic students would have chosen language. His own political ideology requires that economic analysis—in this case, work—supercede [sic] all other forms of analysis. (119)

Shor's pedagogy, as outlined in *Critical Teaching and Everyday Life* and his other books, still influences many compositionists who themselves invoke Freire's name when providing theoretical credit for similar teaching methods—methods now largely called "critical pedagogy" or "radical pedagogy." However, as I hope this discussion has established, Shor's critical pedagogy and concepts of critical teaching abandon some of the basic assumptions of Freirean theory—including and especially its reliance on dialogism—and it is questionable if Shor's pedagogy is in any way liberatory.

Other Liberatory Experiments and Disappointments

Other attempts to apply Freirean dialogic theories to the realities of postsecondary composition and literature classrooms have met with frustration and resistance both on the part of instructors and students (with the possible exception of the work of Kyle Fiore and Nan Elsasser, which I will discuss later). Much of Freire's revolutionary work seems to have devolved into "pedagogical recipes dressed up in the jargon of abstracted progressive labels" (Giroux, *Postcolonialism* 15). Many of these compositionists have been influenced by Shor's misapplication of Freirean theory. While Shor seems satisfied with the outcomes of his courses, some compositionists have written about the problems of transferring Freirean dialogic pedagogy to the postsecondary classroom.

C.H. Knoblauch, who claims to be influenced by Paulo Freire, Henry Giroux, and Ira Shor, does not see the application of Freirean dialogic theory as unproblematically as Shor does. He questions whether liberatory learning can be "anything more than an intellectual game" in most North American universities:

Can the university really serve as a site for radical teaching? What is the meaning of "radical teacher" for faculty in such privileged institutions—paid by the capitalist state, protected from many of the obligations as well as consequences of social action by the speculativeness of academic commitment, engaged in a seemingly trivial dramatization of utopian thought, which the university itself blandly sponsors as satisfying testimony to its own open-mindedness. (15–16)

As an example of the problem he sees, Knoblauch describes his experience with a literature class, an introduction to short

114 *Literacy, Ideology, Dialogue*

prose fiction. The students are assigned a story called "The Lesson" by Toni Cade Bambara, which depicts an excursion by a group of children from Harlem to Manhattan and the Fifth Avenue toy store, F.A.O. Schwartz, known for expensive merchandise (Knoblauch describes the store as "outrageously upscale"). The children are "awed by what they see, particularly by a toy sailboat that costs over a thousand dollars. They talk about what it might mean that some people spend more on a toy than others have to spend in a year for eating and sleeping" (16). The "lesson" is never spelled out in the story; the children cannot agree among themselves about the meaning of their experience, nor does the narrator provide the answer. Knoblauch asks his students for written responses that speculate what the story's lesson might be.

The initial responses can be summarized roughly as follows: the lesson of the story is that if ghetto children work hard enough in school and life, they too will someday be able to purchase such toys. Knoblauch does not engage in a "power struggle over preferable readings" with his students; instead, he copies several of the typical responses on the board and asks the students what values are implicit in their responses to the story. Certain themes emerge from the discussion: "a belief that education is intrinsically liberating and also a belief that hard work leads inevitably to The Good Life" (17). Knoblauch tries to problematize the students' responses by asking other questions: "Why do we take these as true? If they are true for us, are they then true for everyone? Are they, in fact, always true for us? What does experience suggest? What documentation can we discover?" (17–18). Knoblauch is disappointed to report that even after this questioning of values presented in the students' initial responses, the final responses were much the same as the initial ones. The students seemed unable or unwilling to confront such issues as conspicuous consumption, or the fact that many of them could not afford such an expensive toy either, or "a value system that produces an F.A.O. Schwartz in the first place" (18). For the rest of the term, the results were the same.

Knoblauch raises the issue that his are not the working–class students whom Shor describes but come "from the comfortable middle of the American middle class" (12). For Knoblauch, the problem of liberatory teaching is not one of methodology but of the social position of his students:

> The issue here seems to go beyond tactics to a question of the real plausibility of liberatory teaching in circumstances where there is a powerful self–interest, rooted in class advantage, that works actively, if not consciously, against critical reflectiveness. What do my students have to gain from a scrutiny of values and conditions that work to insure their privilege? Why should they struggle with the troubling self–awareness that one course aims to create when the culture of the university as a whole reassures them of their entitlements? (19)

These middle–class students see no need for change; the system, so far anyway, is working in their favor. If they work hard, the students believe, the poor or disadvantaged can overcome their difference and live "normally." Members of the dominant culture often believe, as Knoblauch's students seem to, that people who suffer from poverty, or speak another language, or have other cultural values, are simply deviant; they are not "normal." Freire warns that the oppressors cannot liberate themselves because they see their condition as the norm. The problem of devising a dialogic, liberatory curriculum for students who may not see any need to be liberated is certainly a central issue if one is to claim that a pedagogy is at all liberatory.

I would argue that the method Knoblauch employs in his class was not liberatory and therefore less likely to accomplish the desired outcome to begin with. He never problematizes the concept of a literature class. In all respects, this class is a typical lower-level literature class. The students are asked to write responses to "literature"; they read the material and write essays about what the story, or poem, or play, or novel *means*— or at least the interpretation that, according to their best guess, is going to get them the best grade from this instructor. Knoblauch does nothing to lead students to believe that the risk of any sort of revolutionary thinking expressed on their part would be rewarded. How has he encouraged any kind of real dialogue with his students? Class discussion about issues of privilege and social class certainly does not constitute the kind of dialogic radical pedagogy Freire envisions.

Like Shor, Knoblauch abandons the action side of the praxis dialectic: reflection and action. He never encourages students to write for audiences beyond the classroom. Like Shor, Knoblauch neither offers nor rewards writing addressed to anyone outside the classroom. And furthermore, who outside the classroom would be interested in reading these students' essays about short stories? What reason do these students have to write, except that it is what they have come to expect, unproblematically for both Knoblauch and the students, in a literature class? And not only are the assignments arhetorical, but, as in Shor's pedagogy, there is no true dialogic interaction among equals. What dialogue there is remains between the teacher and the student. The students are writing to receive grades; there is nothing more at stake. These students know that what they write is not as important as what the instructor thinks about what they write. In such a situation, they are unlikely to say anything that risks much controversy. Years of banking education have demonstrated to them that the best way to achieve success, so often defined as good grades, is to do what the instructor wants—even though one may not understand why it is important. Dialogue, true questioning, and critical thinking are so rarely rewarded that students are not likely to engage in them unless they are given clear clues that that is what is expected and that it is "safe" to do so. That is, students need to know that what they say will be taken seriously as a statement of a thinking person and that the instructor and the other students will actually respond and engage in a dialogue. Knoblauch provides none of these conditions in his classroom.

Like Shor, Knoblauch abandons the dialogic aspect of liberatory pedagogy. Since the curriculum is *imposed* on the students rather than determined through dialogic inquiry in partnership with the students, Knoblauch cannot devise a curriculum that reflects the concrete existence of the students' lives or gain any understanding about how his students see the world. One of the problems with this class may be that the students' experience are too far from the ones depicted in the stories they were asked to read. The experience of poverty in America is rarely depicted, even in the news media, in a realistic way. Thus, it is probably difficult for these students to put themselves in the place of the children in Bambara's story. What can Knoblauch's students' know about life in Harlem? What in the students' experiences would make the one depicted in the story comprehensible or meaningful to them?

Of course, any meaningful preliminary dialogic inquiry between Knoblauch and his students to determine the curriculum is not likely to have happened anyway. The constraints endemic to higher education—with its semesters, compartmentalized education, brief class periods—conspire to make such dialogues between professors and students exceedingly difficult. Considering that many writing instructors see their students for approximately three hours per week for approximately fifteen weeks—and may never see these students again—the likelihood of any kind of continuing dialogue between students and instructors dwindles even further. Even the architecture of many institutions would inhibit dialogic pedagogy: large lecture halls and classrooms with small desks set in rows are not conducive to dialogue among students and with the instructor; this arrangement is best suited for sitting quietly and listening as knowledge is transmitted (or "deposited"). The issue of the radical changes necessary in education for dialogic pedagogies to succeed is not often addressed in the contexts of discussions of the adaptability of dialogic, liberatory pedagogy to higher education.

The Irony of North American "Liberatory" Pedagogy

Knoblauch is alarmed by one of the ironies that his experiment with liberatory learning so clearly reveals about much of the applications of liberatory learning in North American higher education:

Typically, when American teachers have appropriated the practices of "critical" pedagogy, they have done so in the name of students perceived to be on the margins of school life, those in remedial programs, those from "minority groups" traditionally excluded from fast academic tracks, those who have dropped out of school. The goal has been to find ways to enfranchise "outsiders," typically by making them more aware of the social realities that constitute their lives; more aware of the means by which power is gained, used, and distributed in the professional and other communities they may wish to enter; more aware of the ways simultaneously to acquire that power and also subvert the structures that objectify prevailing, and debilitating, power arrangements. (14–15)

The irony has been that Freire is often invoked when we search for teaching strategies that will help marginalized students. Those students who have a great deal of trouble with literacy as it is defined by higher education and who therefore are often unable to gain access to the social benefits and power that higher education can confer are considered ripe for empowerment. However, the concept of empowerment so often linked with Freire and radical pedagogy may in reality be no more than indoctrination into what Freire calls the oppressor class. In most of the North American applications of liberatory learning, none of the social systems that marginalize groups of students in the first place are in any way displaced. Liberatory learning is often used to bring marginalized groups into the structures of traditional education—leaving those structures largely unchanged. Knoblauch is concerned, along with Giroux, that when liberatory learning is applied only in remedial education, literacy then is conceived in terms of a deficit theory of learning.

If dialogic pedagogy is to transform our students into active agents, then perhaps we also need to be prepared for the revolutionary transformation and reform that that dialogue is likely to entail. Neither Knoblauch nor I have any easy answer to this profound problem in the American education system, which as Giroux argues threatens everyone's access as citizens to active, democratic public life (Giroux, *Literacy* 5).[7] In such a democratic public life, dialogue is the way that differences are addressed and that the structure of power and hierarchy can be perceived, addressed, and perhaps transformed.

Victor Villanueva, Jr. supplies a partial answer to these questions of power hierarchy. For two semesters, Villanueva observed Floyd—a pseudonym for a "Freire-trained teacher, freed from usual curricular or institutional constraints"—teach writing in a "midwestern, not-for-profit private school aimed exclusively at low-income adolescents and young adults who had been locked out of traditional public schools but wanted back in" (251). Villanueva concludes that even under almost ideal conditions for dialogic pedagogy, certain factors limit the success of this method. He argues convincingly that American Freireistas underestimate the power of hegemony in their classrooms.

Hegemony, a Gramscian concept, is central to Villanueva's work:

> Hegemony represents the ways in which ruling classes affect a society's moral and intellectual leadership so as to have the rulers' interests appear the interests of other social groups. That is, the dominant classes exploit commonalities between their ideologies and the ideologies of other classes. As a result, those in what Gramsci calls subaltern positions see themselves as serving their own interests. And they are, to some extent. They also see that they are serving the interests of the dominant classes but self-interest overrides. (250–51)

Hegemony in this sense inherently encompasses contradictions. For instance, women have long known that many of their interests and those of the male-dominant group are in conflict, yet many continue to foster male domination because of the benefits that accrue to them. So contradictions exist within belief systems. The oppressed, in this case the students, are complicitous with the oppressor in their own oppression, thereby making it doubly difficult to perceive the ways in which the system oppresses them.

According to Villanueva, American Freirean educators have failed in their pedagogies to account for the contradictions left unexamined within their own and within students' belief systems. This is a problem in American classrooms in a way that it is not in many of the situations in which Freire worked:

Freire's critical literacy at the sites of recent revolutions is directed almost exclusively at encountering criticism, at countering hegemony. There, Freire must focus on having the previously dominated discard the elements of their ideologies that had served their oppressors. But here, in America, where revolution moves slowly; here in the American college composition classroom, where our interchanges with students are relativelyshort . . . counterhegemony cannot be easily sold. (251)

Floyd, like Shor and Knoblauch, purposely chooses propaganda over dialogue. In this way, contradictions in the hegemony never emerge. As with the other writing instructors, the dialogic nature of praxis is abandoned. The result is that Floyd had only limited success. Floyd's methods worked on those students "already predisposed to his worldview," and the others remained as they were (256). As Villanueva observes:

Those students who saw the hope of black people in religion, wrote of salvation through prayer and devotion, of future good in suffering now. Those who followed the tenets of nonviolent protest wrote of the steady progress black folks have known since the struggles of Martin Luther King. Those who believed in simple, undirected opposition wrote of "blue-eyed devils." The students had not been politically affected in the manner Floyd had apparently intended. (256)

Villanueva goes on to point out that certain belief systems, myths that obstruct liberatory praxis, were evident in the classroom and were even reinforced in subtle ways by the instructor. These myths or themes (such as education leads to success, and individual achievement leads to the betterment of society through the progress of a collection of individuals) would have had to have emerged in the class and have been examined in a joint, dialogic effort on the part of Floyd and his students if they were to loosen their obstructive hold on the students' views of the world.

Any collective gathering for revolutionary action is simply not an option because enough blacks get through the system for the perception that "gains are being made" to be maintained:

> Individual achievement is sold as the betterment of society through the progress of a collection of individuals. Such progress undermines Floyd's zeal, negates Floyd's call to arms. One successful figure—Floyd—espousing the students' abilities for success, is not likely to persuade those students that a revolutionary consciousness is a better definition of success than the possibility for individual fame or fortune. (257)

The myth of individual achievement should in this case become a generative theme. It is a limit–situation that, so far, not many American Freireistas have acknowledged, much less challenged.

Thus, Villanueva agrees with my contention that few of the "American Freireistas" actually employ dialogic, liberatory learning, though they claim to. In all the examples discussed so far, the dialogic nature of the pedagogy has been ignored, short–circuiting the dialectic between reflection and action that leads students to critical literacy. Once dialogic inter-change is absent, radical pedagogy ceases to be both radical and liberatory. Dialogism is the engine that drives true Freirean pedagogy, and the frustrated attempts of compositionists to employ radical pedagogy minus dialogism serve as telling testimony of this fact.

Returning the Dialogic to Radical Pedagogy

A possible exception to this account of failed experiments is Kyle Fiore and Nan Elsasser's account of Elsasser's college-level writing class at the College of the Bahamas. Although it could be argued that her students were not typical North American college students (they were all adult black women), Elsasser's course was taught within institutional constraints and still seemed to produce remarkable results. Unlike the attempts at radical pedagogy discussed so far, Elsasser to a much greater extent did maintain the dialogic aspects of liberatory learning. Her theoretical framework for the course was drawn equally from Vygotsky and Freire:

These scholars intrigued us because they believe writing involves both cognitive skills and social learnings. Their approaches parallel and complement each other. Vygotsky explores students' internal learning process. Freire emphasizes the impact of external social reality. . . . Vygotsky's work clarifies the complex process of writing. He postulates that learning to write involves the mastery of cognitive skills and the development of new social understandings. . . . Vygotsky explains that to transform the inner speech symbols to written text, [students] must consciously step outside the shorthand of [their] thoughts and mentally enter the social context [they share] with [their] reader. (88)

Elsasser introduces Vygotsky's theory of inner speech to illustrate for students the difference between what they think and what must be written.

She begins this process by using simple word association exercises: "Comparing their responses to trigger words such as *sex, home, work,* the women start to see that even at this most basic level they categorize and store information in various ways" (91). They spend the first three weeks on the these types of exercises, ending each class period by transforming their lists of associated words into public prose.

The next assignment is ingenious in its ability to accomplish several goals at once. Elsasser needs an assignment that "will stress the value of personal knowledge, break down the dichotomy between personal and classroom knowledge, and require explicit elaboration" (91). She asks students to write an essay entitled "What You Need to Know to Live in the Bahamas." This assignment serves other purposes as well. Unlike much of the writing assigned in college–level composition classes, this assignment could actually be interesting to an audience outside the classroom; it has a clear rhetorical purpose. In addition, it provides Elsasser with information about the daily lives of the students that otherwise she has no access to, as she herself is a newcomer to the islands. Responses to the assignment become part of the dialogic, two–way inquiry into the everyday lives of her students.

The students have some trouble with this first extended assignment, largely having to do with audience. But during the extended dialogue in class, the students begin to emerge from their personal perspectives as they discuss and critique each other's drafts. By the end of the sequence of classes that develop this assignment, Elsasser is able to say, "Gradually they start to investigate their environment. Before, they passively received knowledge. Now, they pursue it" (92). In a remarkably short time Elsasser's students have become subjects, and it is largely through her extensive reliance on dialogic interchange that they are able to advance so rapidly.

Like Shor's students, these writers are launched into an inquiry about their everyday lives. However, unlike Shor's students, Elsasser allows the inquiry to follow the students' interests, and she resists imposing any particular curriculum content on them. She admits that she is unable to engage in prolonged dialogic research to reveal the generative themes that would be the most meaningful to her students. She solves this problem by asking them to "select three issues from their daily lives that they would like to talk, read, and write about for the semester" (92). They vote on the topics presented and select the topic of marriage, which turns out to be an effective generative theme for this class. As Elsasser observes:

> This theme effects their lives economically, socially, and emotionally. Ninety percent of these women have been raised by two parents in traditional Bahamian homes. Seventy-five percent are now mothers. Two-thirds of these mothers are single parents totally responsible for their children's physical and emotional well-being. (92)

The women then move into small groups and discuss what subtopics their investigation should cover and construct an outline that includes housework, divorce, sexuality, and domestic violence. Elsasser then sets out to provide readings that will elaborate these themes for the students.

They spend the rest of the semester in a dialogic co-investigation of their subtopics. Elsasser provides articles related to each of the subtopics and only the background information necessary to clarify any unfamiliar concepts presented in the essays. Elsasser describes what happens during these weeks:

During our investigation students pass through three distinct phases as they hone their abilities to examine, critique, and write about marriage. They elaborate their own experience more skillfully, and they perceive stronger links between their own lives and the larger social context. They reach outside their own experience to seek new sources of knowledge. Finally, they become critically conscious of the way society affects their lives, and they begin to use writing as a means of intervening in their own social environment. (93)

These students intervene in their social environment by writing an open letter to the men of the Bahamas that was eventually carried in both daily newspapers. These students also planned to continue to meet together "to read about women in other countries, broaden their understandings, and write a resource book for Bahamian women" (103).

As you can see, the course can be quite different when the dialogic nature of the pedagogy is maintained. The students and the instructor engaged in an inquiry about an aspect of the concrete, material existence of the students' lives. Unlike the classes of Shor, Floyd, and Knoblauch, in Elsasser's class it was the students' interests that guided the inquiry; Elsasser did not impose a curriculum on them. Unlike the other liberatory courses discribed, in Elsasser's class the students' writing became rhetorical and social, eventually addressing their community and beginning a dialogue with others outside the classroom. The students did indeed begin to perceive their "limit situations" as challenges to be transformed. They experienced the excitement of writing that has consequences in the world—an experience that many college-level writing courses do not offer students. Most of Elsasser's students received a "B" on the department exit examination. The school's fail rate the year before Elsasser arrived was "forty–five to sixty–percent" (90). So Elsasser's students did well above the average.

Experiments in radical pedagogy are continuing. The University of Nothern Arizona and Mount St. Mary's College in Emmitsburg, Maryland have developed first–year composition courses that use the students' experiences as first–year students as the subject of the course.[8] However, it would seem that the general failure of Freirean radical pedagogy in U.S. college and university classrooms is directly proportional to the instructor's failure to intitiate and maintain a truly dialogic pedagogy. In addition, postsecondary education offers no mechanisms for sustaining and supporting the dialogue and the energy for change that a truly liberatory pedagogy on this level would generate. Since students must continue in their programs, taking a different set of classes each term, any communities that they might form would be under a great deal of pressure from the system to deteriorate. Clearly, Freirean pedagogy relies on dialogue to ensure the liberatory nature of the educative process. For Freire, dialogue is the means to critical consciousness, or conscientization. It is only in dialogue with others that students are able to confront the complexity of posed problems and to work out solutions on their own, thereby placing themselves in active subject positions. In short, dialogue is the true engine of radical pedagogy as articulated by its originators. When the dialogic process breaks down, the radical transformative nature of education is lost.

Notes

1. I have decided to quote verbatim from Freire's *Pedagogy of the Oppressed*, however I am aware of the sexist bias of the language and call it to the reader's attention.

2. But as Freire continually points out, the oppressors, too, are dehumanized by their participation in oppression. The struggle of the oppressed to free themselves and become more fully human will necessarily involve the liberation of the oppressors as well.

3. For example, Freire states that *domination* is the generative theme of our epoch; another that is characteristic of many societies is social and economic *underdevelopment*.

4. Shor fails to address one key problem: when students don't speak a standard dialect, where does the self-correction come from?

5. See Myers, Ashton–Jones, and Smit.

6. Shor has written a Marxist critique of community college education. See "The Working Class Goes to College" in *Critical Teaching*.

7. See also Giroux, *Schooling and the Struggle for Public Life* for a discussion of the role of schooling in democracy.

8. The Northern Arizona experiment is briefly mentioned in Villaneuva. I have knowledge of the course at Mount St. Mary's from personal discussions with the program director, Byron Stay.

Postmodern Views of Discourse and Dialogism

The expressivist, social constructionist, and liberatory perspectives assume varying and sometimes contradictory notions of dialogism. Yet, all of these perspectives are considered part of composition's "process paradigm." Recently, several compositionists have challenged the process paradigm, attempting to institute a postprocess, postmodern pedagogy. These compositionists have been heavily influenced by deconstruction and other poststructuralist theories.

Because attempts to devise a postmodern theory and pedagogy are relatively recent, such models are only in the process of being formulated; scholars have not yet reached consensus as to exactly what elements a postmodern pedagogy should necessarily include. Nevertheless, it seems clear that it is concerned, first, with power relations within the classroom and within any discourse situation. In addition, like the social constructionist perspective, a postmodern pedagogy conceives of truth and knowledge not as stable and determinable but as always contingent and dependent on local context. Knowledge, like language, can be understood, or have meaning, only within unique communicative situations in which two or more people engage in a dialogue about an object or idea. This dialogue is open–ended, one in which truth is only provisionally established, and serves as an invitation to further dialogue.

Such a radically new epistemology has deep implications for how pedagogy is constructed.

In the last five years, a small but increasing number of published works have attempted to make connections between poststructuralist theory and composition pedagogy or theory. Three figures, however, are especially noteworthy: Gregory Ulmer, who posits a rationale for a postmodern pedagogy in general; William A. Covino, who has attempted to develop a postmodern composition pedagogy; and Thomas Kent, who through a sustained effort has worked to devise a postprocess, postmodern theory for composition studies.

Gregory Ulmer and Applied Grammatology

Perhaps one of the most well known and oft-cited works applying deconstructive theory to pedagogy, particularly writing pedagogy, is Gregory Ulmer's *Applied Grammatology: Post(e)-Pedagogy from Jacques Derrida to Joseph Beuys*. Ulmer attempts to replace the word *deconstruction* with *grammatology*, which he sees as a more inclusive term, "embracing both deconstruction and 'writing' (understood not only in the special sense of textualist *écriture*, but also in the sense of a compositional practice)" (x). Like theorists concerned with radical pedagogy, Ulmer, and by extension other deconstructionists, is concerned with power relations within the classroom. Ulmer attempts to bypass the traditional notion of teaching as the transmission of knowledge, of cultural and intellectual reproduction, and to institute instead a pedagogy that is self-interested—that is, one in which both the teacher and students are constantly aware of their epistemological positions and personal assumptions and preconceptions. Ulmer sees traditional education as subscribing to a Hegelian model in which the teacher is both an authority figure and a model whom the students must imitate. The Hegelian perspective assumes that truth, knowledge, is always absolute and external to specific situations and human relations and that the teacher, as the authority, transmits this truth to his or her charges. In addition, the Hegelian model, according to Ulmer, privileges verbal discourse at the expense of other kinds of discourse, such as what Derrida often refers to as "picto–ideo–phonographic Writing."

Ulmer wishes to deconstruct this traditional Hegelian model and to make pedagogy reflect the intellectual paradigm shift that is occurring in the arts: the cultural and intellectual shift from modernism to postmodernism. Citing Michel Serres, Ulmer argues that it is necessary "to bring educational practice into line with contemporary epistemology—to help pedagogy negotiate the same paradigm shift that altered the arts and sciences at the beginning of our century, leaving pedagogy behind in the age of Hegel" (163). He sees one of the objectives of grammatology as hastening the end of the age of positivism (167). Thus, pedagogy in the deconstructive view is "committed to change rather than to reproduction" (162).

In the Hegelian instructional paradigm, the teacher's role is "that of model and authority, a concrete embodiment of the ideal self with which the student must identify (from Socrates to Freud and beyond, transference is an important element in pedagogical effect)" (166). The student's role is to imitate this ideal self. Inevitably, the power relationship that develops then is that of master and disciple. Thus, the student is understood as always "not yet" a self; the student imitates the teacher in a process of becoming, as practice for some future, emerging self that is like the instructor.

Because the Hegelian model is based on an assumed universality and stability of truth (and, therefore, knowledge), it is by definition authoritative, "in its very nature a kind of symbolic violence" (169). Like his or her students, "the teacher is indoctrinated to believe he [or she] can only repeat a message rather than produce one himself" or herself (171). True invention has no place in this model of learning. Translating the Hegelian model specifically to the composition classroom, students never engage in real discourse; they never "invent," but are continually imitating discourse in preparation for "real" communication.

In place of the Hegelian model, Ulmer wishes to view the classroom in theatrical terms—a play in which the master's and disciples' roles are deconstructed and replaced with a new scene in which the "pedagogy of communication" is acted differently. In such a radically altered pedagogical environment, the classroom is "*a place of invention rather than of reproduction*" (164). It is a paradoxical pedagogy because it assumes a problematic relationship to truth, attempting to teach the "unteachable *relation* to truth." Poststructuralism "puts in question the very notion of truth, in which the claims of truth to objectivity and neutrality are exposed as effects of an apparatus of power" (168). In other words, any truth claim is already implicated in the power relationships of those who benefit from or are disadvantaged by the truth claim's particular version of "reality." The new pedagogy understands knowledge as "invented" in "the scene of life," that is, as continually unfolding in the play of discourse, as an open–ended, dialogic process with only provisional closure (167).

In order for this scene of life or "place of invention" to materialize in the classroom, students and teachers must conceptualize their respective roles differently. As Ulmer claims, "The new pedagogy, then, must attempt to do away with the undesirable pedagogical effect of discipleship precisely because it generates disciplines and authorities" (173). This new scene replaces the authoritative "professorial discourse—the literate mastery of the word—[which] . . . condemns the teacher to 'theatrical monologue and virtuoso exhibition'" with a kind of performance that calls attention to the meaning created by that setting. Like Antonin Artaud's "theater of cruelty," in which the separation between stage and auditorium, actor and audience are blurred and, therefore, call attention to their meaning in the setting and attempt to bring immediate experience into participation with the represented experience of the play, this pedagogy calls into question the meaning of the setting of the traditional classroom. When this separation between lecturer and disciple is bridged and the meaning of the classroom setting is called into question, then the difference between representing experience and "real" experience becomes a meaningless separation and can be done away with. In the theater of cruelty, theater "is not representation [of life] but 'life itself'" where the separation between "actor and audience, master and pupil" are transformed and then erased (172, 174, 175).

In this new scene of teaching, the message is replaced by the medium as the most significant pedagogical feature. A postmodern classroom, then, would be a place where life itself is enacted or played out directly—unobstructed by a master/disciple power relationship and settings that compel students to represent themselves as those "not yet," and, therefore, preventing students from engaging in invention.

Ulmer's conception of postmodern pedagogy as a kind of "avant–guard performance art" explicitly links pedagogy and invention and, thus, pedagogy and rhetoric (174). Ulmer writes:

> An application of grammatology to teaching, in other words, involves a rethinking of the "space" in which the discourse of ideas takes place. Given that grammatological presentations are neither reproductions of reality nor revelations of the real, it is clear that grammatology

> *involves a displacement of educational transmissions from*
> *the domain of truth to that of invention.* (179)

Thus, postmodern pedagogy enacts the scene of knowledge and this enactment involves the rhetorical art of invention—specifically, "of searching through the places or topoi to find material for one's own text" (179). One's own text does not unfold by passively, silently listening to a delivered monologue of received knowledge but through active participation in the process of inquiry and, hence, in the production of knowledge.

Following Ulmer's use of theatrical metaphors, the scene of writing, then, implies a dialogic relationship among the actors or participants in the scene taking place in the composition classroom. As in the radical pedagogy discussed in chapter three, the students as well as the teacher are given the speaking parts. In this new play, as in radical pedagogy, the master is denied the sole authority to speak and power to represent. A deconstructive composition pedagogy, involved as it is with situationality, should entail some form of dialogism at the scene of writing. Active participation in the production of knowledge necessarily entails dialogue with others. Even in the most isolated and private moments of composing, writing is dialogic. The self cannot remain singular and autonomous and write, because writing necessarily involves the pluralization of self into at least two others: writer and audience. The scene of writing is defined by Derrida as a scene in which one attempts to communicate with an other that is not present. Dialogue with an other, even an absent other such as an imagined audience, is necessary to the scene of writing.[1]

Ulmer's own continued explorations of postmodern pedagogy have led him to investigate ways of incorporating other kinds of signification, like video, into discourse education.[2] However, I believe Ulmer gives compositionists a place to ask, as he himself finally does, "How might this new pedagogy actually be performed?" Using theoretical justification based in postmodern theories of language, several compositionists have tried to answer this question by employing various versions of dialogic interaction and performative methodology in composition pedagogy.

(En)acting a Postmodern Pedagogy

One of the major pedagogies that attempts to apply postmodern theory to the composition class is the work of William A. Covino. Covino advocates a pedagogy in which students write open–ended dialogues in order to gain knowledge of multiple viewpoints. In *The Art of Wondering: A Revisionist Return to the History of Rhetoric*, Covino takes a revisionist look at the history of rhetorical theory from a postmodern perspective. He claims that this perspective asks us to recognize that "all writing is interpretive: history or poetry or philosophy or journalism represses something in order to say something else" (2). That is, in any writing situation, we make choices from available facts and according to what information is important or serves our purpose or audience best. This filtering process of filling in the gaps from missing details and choosing among available information or among viewpoints involves interpretation.

Covino looks back at the scholarship in rhetorical history, focusing on what has been repressed in Plato, Aristotle, and Cicero and demonstrating how they anticipate "overtly renegade advocates of open discourse: Montaigne, Vico, Hume, Byron, and DeQuincey" (3). Covino argues that the traditional readings of the classical canon have "reified their works into lists of rules and principles" (33). Covino's rereading of Plato, Aristotle, and Cicero recovers the aspects of their works that value ambiguity, open-endedness, and multiple perspectives, what Covino calls "the art of wondering":

> Techniques, rules, and formulas for composing and arranging *finished* discourse fill the handbooks that comprise the mainstream tradition. The "forgotten" rhetors are those who elaborate Plato's conception of rhetoric as (I will argue) an art of wondering, and writing as a mode of *avoiding* rather than *intending* closure. (9)

The pedagogical implications of Covino's postmodern reading of rhetorical history would necessitate, according to Covino, the addition of unconventional genres such as dialogue and drama into the writing curriculum, genres that shift emphasis away from the demand for closure common to many academic forms of discourse, forms he calls "formalist-objective." Covino defines formalist-objective discourse as writing that places "emphasis on a clear thesis, a clear purpose, and a focus on only the facts relevant to the thesis and purpose, [writing that] encourages us to make a final decision" (*Forms* 61). It "presents the world and each phenomenon in it as a *definite structure of elements*. . . . So the function of the formalist-objective writing is to take what's very complicated—and *everything* is—and make it simpler"; it presents a "vision of the world" (4). Related to the Hegelian model that Ulmer wishes to deconstruct, formalist-objective writing emphasizes the *stability* of knowledge and the world (3).

In contrast, Covino advocates allowing the student to explore multiple perspectives without necessarily having to come to any closure or proclaim a final decision, without having to "take a stand:"

> I have in mind a student writing . . . [that] is informed by associational thinking, a repertory of harlequin changes,

by the resolution that resolution itself is anathema. This writer writes to see what happens.

I am not suggesting that students should learn to trade clarity for obscurity (a trade that some postmodern writers have been accused of making). I am suggesting that they should trade certainty for ambiguity, trade preservative writing for investigative writing, trade conclusions for "counterinduction." The climate is right for writing teachers to point out that the world is a drama of people and ideas and that writing is how we consistently locate and relocate ourselves in the play. (*Art of Wondering* 130)

Rather than taking a positive stance for or against an issue, student writing should be exploratory and self-reflexive, should ask questions rather than provide answers. Clearly, Covino is trying to enact the type of postmodern pedagogy (applied grammatology) that Ulmer and other theoreticians are calling for, in that, in Covino's class, knowledge is understood to unfold as a "drama of people and ideas" and students are expected to participate in this inventive process.

In "Defining Advanced Composition," Covino explicitly describes the kind of dialogic writing assignment he has in mind. This assignment is designed to encourage students to "keep an issue alive." He provides the following as an example of a dialogic writing assignment.

The Dialogue

Topic: An unexplored, unsettled, ambiguous, or confusing element of a subject that matters.

Characters:
  1) Three experts on your topic, each with a different viewpoint. These are *real* experts, with significant

reputations and published work (which you have reviewed).

2) Two curious, critical, undecided students with substantial interest in the topic.

Constraints:

1) No one makes stupid or characteristic statements.

2) No one wins; that is, no one view finally seems more intelligent, persuasive, or inclusive than the others.

3) Each character speaks at least three times, for at least half a page at each turn.

4) The experts occasionally quote or paraphrase themselves or each other; each character is familiar with the others' published work.

5) No one delivers "throwaway" lines or transitions, such as "How True, tell me more."

6) Each character's words are planned and crafted. This is a thoughtful, deliberate writing, neither spontaneous nor casual, as if the characters had revised and edited their spoken words for publication (see, for instance, the occasional dialogues that have appeared in the "Forum" section of recent issues of *Harper's*). (120)

According to Covino this writing task

insists upon *substance* while discouraging a particular *stance*. Further, with its emphasis on planned discourse, it encourages license without vagueness; thus, students are warned against words which "tumble out under the blindest accident of the moment" . . . they must create a . . . common sense, by enlarging the lexicon of viewpoints that comprise human history and decisions . . . they must set aside conviction to practice rhetoric. (122)

This assignment asks students to defer or suppress conviction. Instead, the students' task is to explore all sides of an issue rather than to persuade a reader to accept any particular view of the issue.

Covino develops this pedagogy further in a first-year composition textbook, *Forms of Wondering: A Dialogue on Writing, for Writers*, constructed as a book-length dialogue. It contains no chapter headings; instead, it reads like one, long playscript. Covino creates nine voices, all aspects of himself, that are the main "actors": Covino the Sophist, Covino the Expediter, Covino the Epistemologist, Covino the Writing Teacher, Covino the TV Watcher, Covino the Radical, Covino the Administrator, and Covino the Textbook Writer. In keeping with Ulmer's recommendation to create a pedagogy that is performance-based and self-aware, Covino uses these voices to *perform* for students the kind of writing he is advocating, and they allow him to display his pedagogy's theoretical framework. In addition, Covino introduces other voices in the form of full-length examples of dialogic writing, including a transcript of a "Donahue" program, an essay by Montaigne, all of Plato's *Phaedrus*, and student essays in response to the assignments.

Sometimes Covino's voices come into conflict: the radical and the administrator sometimes vigorously interrupt the other voices; other times, the expeditor will impatiently provide a summary or ask a pointed question. At times the conflict demonstrates advantages, limits, and dangers of some of Covino's theoretical positions. In this way, the book is self-critical and is able to explore implications of its own theoretical premises—something that most other textbooks do not attempt.

Covino's writing assignments ask students to compose dialogues or drama; all the assignments call for voices in dialogue.

For instance, one assignment asks students to write a two-act play on a single word, exploring all of the connotations of the concept.

Despite Covino's conscious attempt to employ a postmodern dialogic pedagogy, his curriculum suffers from many of the pitfalls that postmodern pedagogy claims to avoid. In Covino's model, the student is in dialogue with the instructor rather than with the self (as in the expressivist model), or with other students (as in the social constructionist model), or with the world (as in the Freirean model). The audience for the writing is the instructor. The assignments do not ask students to address their dialogues to audiences beyond the composition classroom. The textbook does not ask students' peers to act as audience, although the book does not specifically prohibit students' reading and commenting on each other's papers. Collaborative learning, conceived as peer-revision activities, is not mentioned in Covino's work.

One obvious criticism of Covino's pedagogy is that it fails to engage students in dialogue beyond the classroom or prepare them for such writing situations. Covino anticipates this criticism through the voice of the Expeditor:

> The "open essay" might be good practice if our goal were training students to write for the *New Yorker* magazine, or other publications—quite rare—that feature "voluble" essayists. But we cannot deny our responsibility to equip students for the writing they will be called upon to produce in the postgraduate, professional world. *Like it or not, an orderly, decisive presentation of relevant facts is what counts as good writing in college, in graduate school, in business, law, medicine, science, and politics.* (294–95)

Clearly, Covino realizes that the forms of discourse that he is teaching are in many ways at odds with the institutions in which students produce them. A student's professor of history, social science, and even literature may not accept this form of dialogic writing as fulfilling the requirements for an assignment. Students may never be asked to write in this manner again and, in fact, could be penalized for such writing.

Covino counters this criticism in several places in the textbook itself. First, he acknowledges, again in the words of the Expediter, that dialogic writing and thinking work "well as *preparation for a well-informed decision*" (84). In this way Covino's course becomes a course in *inventio*, exploration in preparation for some unnamed, future time when an informed decision about issues will be necessary. It is practice for when it may really count. In this way, the course is arhetorical: the student's writing addresses only the instructor for the purpose of demonstrating that they can do what Covino asks of them. Who would write or read such documents? Under what circumstances would someone decide to write in this manner? Clearly, some writers do write such nontraditional forms, but this happens in limited situations that not many students, if the past is any indication, will choose outside of their academic careers.

Covino, however, also argues that dialogic writing *is* practice for the world beyond the classroom, especially in the "information age." Covino's Sophist argues

that the future belongs to those with the ability to use technology to manipulate word patterns and thought patterns. Throughout her book, *In the Age of the Smart Machine*, Shoshana Zuboff of the Harvard Business School points out that computer technology gives business instant access not only to data banks of relevant information but also to programs that graph and chart and reassemble the data in different configurations, relating it to other data so that new relationships and new ideas become possible. Flexible writers who are practiced at looking at words and concepts from a lot of angles, whose *purpose* is to *play with meanings and concepts*, will be in great demand for important positions in business and industry. (62–63)

Covino's Radical quickly interrupts and extends the conversation to issues of social good beyond the Sophist's claim of producing acceptable workers for corporations. He worries that Covino the Sophist is not concerned about the values inherent in the ideas these corporate word manipulators will create:

> I do believe that dialectical thinking and writing can be liberating, but not when it's placed in the service of greed. The right use of writing is for *resisting* greed and narrow-mindedness, for developing greater sympathy for lives and cultures that remain misunderstood and unappreciated. This means keeping an open mind; this means trying to understand and articulate different points of view; this means accepting that history and culture and human life are always changing; this means that what seemed like a good idea yesterday should be questioned and reconsidered today; this means that creating ten possible solutions to a problem is better than creating one, and twenty is better than ten, but it does *not* mean that all ideas are equally good, or equally respectable. (63)

In this volley of voices, Covino illustrates the dialogic nature of critical inquiry, demonstrating how an exploration of multiple perspectives encourages critical thinking; Covino hopes students will come to value multiple perspectives.

This pedagogy frames college-level composition courses in much broader terms than it is normally encountered within the scope of the mission of higher education. In the words of Covino the Administrator, "There's a widespread belief, within the university and among mainstream citizens, that learning to write is not a political or philosophical issue, as it is for other voices in this dialogue. *Learning to write is, simply, mastering standard structures and rules so we can adapt to the demands of adult life*" (63). Covino the Sophist adds the corrective to this "robotic" view of writing: "The robot is the obedient, well-trained employee who sends out only approved form letters, the human is the writer who realizes that formulas and formats for communication are severely limiting" (64).

Covino wants us to believe that dialogic writing will provide transferable skills beyond the writing classroom: if students carry on with Covino's project, they will be better informed about the important issues that they must make decisions about because they value and know how to gather information from many perspectives. They will have practice in reformulating and reconceiving information into new configurations that may lead to new information and new solutions to problems. On the other hand, as Covino knows, the student will find little further reinforcement for the writing practices he or she learns in Covino's dialogic writing class. These concepts of the writing classroom, according to Covino's Administrator, "fly in the faces of my colleagues, and the administrators of the university, and the elected state officials who have deliberated about the mission of higher education" (63). For this reason, Covino's pedagogy can only be part of a larger, balanced project in which students learn a variety of genres and write in a variety of rhetorical situations.

In short, Covino's project has mixed success as a truly postmodern, dialogic pedagogy. He partly succeeds in inventing a postmodern pedagogy in that he understands knowledge as an open–ended process of unfolding that requires the participation of many voices—as he says, a drama of people and ideas. In their writing, students are asked to avoid the closure that assumes that knowledge is stable and universal. Also, Covino's pedagogy is self-aware, because the voices of the textbook continually reflect on and reevaluate the underlying theoretical assumptions of the pedagogy. Nevertheless, Covino's pedagogy fails in several important ways. First, it does not question the classroom setting as a scene of writing and, as a result, the students retain the status of Ulmer's "not yets." Their writing always remains practice for some future coming to be, a conceptual status that the postmodern classroom would like to deconstruct. The scene of writing remains traditionally Hegelian and, in many ways, monologic in that the students never engage in dialogue with any actual others, and, hence, their writing never gains the status of communication, understood as communicating meaning in order to have an effect in the world.

Moreover, Covino fails to formulate a truly dialogic pedagogy. Although students are asked to use forms of discourse that enact dialogical situations, the situation in which the students are writing remains monologic. The interaction in the classroom is primarily between instructor and student; students do not engage in dialogue with each other or with others outside the classroom. Consequently, the discourse cannot become public and rhetorical because it is unable to elicit a response. The discourse is produced primarily to be evaluated for the purpose of assigning grades. So, while Covino's pedagogy claims to be dialogic and postmodern it is both only in limited ways. Thus, despite Covino's major attempt to construct a postmodern pedagogy, the most important work in postmoderrnism and composition has not been in the development of pedagogy, but, rather, in scholarship concerned with discourse theory, especially the work of Thomas Kent.

Toward a Paralogic Rhetoric

Thomas Kent moves composition theory closer to a postmodern and fundamentally dialogic perspective in his investigation of the work of several prominent poststructuralist philosophers whose work deals with epistemology, language, and communication. Although his work draws from time to time on Jacques Derrida, Jean François Lyotard, and others, he deals primarily with the theories of American analytic philosopher Donald Davidson. Kent believes that Davidson's theory of communicative interaction has significant implications for composition studies. Kent represents the general direction in which composition studies appears to be moving. Increasingly, compositionists are investigating theories of communication that elaborate on the dialogic nature of spoken and written discourse to explain how discourse is produced and analyzed.

Kent claims that writing and reading involve a hermeneutic activity, that is, "the interpretation of an another's language code." Readers and writers engage in what Kent calls "hermeneutic guessing." In producing discourse, Kent argues, invention is not the primary and most fundamental activity. Prior to invention, a writer makes a "hermeneutic guess" about the reader's code. Writers make these guesses because, although we may be guided by the conventionality of discourse communities, no *exact* match between the writer's hermeneutic strategy and the reader's is ever possible. Thus, this hermeneutic activity

> requires the skillful manipulation of signs, and this skill already presupposes language know–how that cannot be codified. Because they require (1) skill that cannot be codified and (2) skillful guessing that cannot be reduced to a formal method or technique, both discourse production

and discourse analysis include a crucial hermeneutic act
that is unsystematic, nonconventional, and paralogic in
nature. ("Paralogic Hermeneutics" 30)

Thus, Kent asks, if reading and writing cannot be reduced to a
codifiable system that predicts discourse activities with any
certainty, how can these activities be described and how can
they be taught? In order to understand Kent's answer to this
crucial question, we first need to trace the theoretical claims of
poststructuralist philosophy and how those claims challenge
some of the most basic assumptions of contemporary
composition theory.

Kent sees his major project as moving composition theory
beyond the process paradigm. He views social constructionism
as part of the process paradigm, and a large part of his critique
deals with its problems. Kent sees two major problems with
social constructionist theory: its reliance on the concepts of
convention and *discourse community*. Kent points out that the
major theories of composition involve some fundamental
notion of "convention." Social convention is, of course, a
fundamental assumption of social constructionist epistemology, as discussed in chapter two. For the social constructionist,
according to Kent, "socially constructed conventions constitute all that we can know about reality. . . . Our ability to
produce discourse becomes contingent on our fundamental
ability to understand our social and historical situation" ("Beyond System" 497). Social conventions then are understood as
the means by which discourse is comprehended. Although
language is thought to be conventional by most contemporary
language philosophers, Davidson and Derrida seriously question the assumption that language is convention–bound. Kent
argues that the critiques provided by Davidson and Derrida
question not only our understanding of the nature of language

but also the very foundation of contemporary rhetoric; such critiques suggest, therefore, that perhaps our notion of rhetoric needs to be reformulated.

Davidson surveys those language theories that claim that the connection between words and what they mean is conventional, and he then argues against them. Kent concludes, along with Davidson, that

> our social conditioning does not provide us with a store of language conventions from which we draw when we wish to communicate something; social conditioning simply ensures us "that we may, up to a point, assume that the same method of interpretation that we use for others, or that we assume others use for us, will work for a new speaker." In a Gadamerian sense, social conditioning provides us with a horizon within which we test out our interpretive possibilities when we encounter a speaker or a text, and the fit of one hermeneutic strategy with another can never be prescribed in advance. At best, then, social conventions represent only one kind of hermeneutic element that helps us communicate. ("Beyond System" 502)

Thus, according to Davidson, the concept of convention serves as a "practical crutch" aiding interpretation, but it is not the fundamental or necessary theoretical construct that allows us to understand how meaning is communicated by discourse. Davidson argues that a more illuminating way of looking at the process of communicating meaning involves what he calls "radical interpretation." Kent explains:

> Radical interpretation means that we employ our knowledge of a language to make guesses about what speakers and writers desire to communicate, and no

formal method may be established to ensure that our
guesses will be correct. A knowledge of conventions—
linguistic or otherwise—only helps make us better guessers.
(502)

Kent is not denying that language conventions exist and to a
point aid in speakers' and writers' attempts to communicate,
but instead, argues that convention is not the foundation upon
which the communication of meaning rests. Whatever it is that
allows us to understand each other is not recognizable as a
stable, unified system or as "conventional" in any axiomatic
way.

Kent draws on Derrida to elaborate further his claims and
corroborate those of Davidson. While Davidson confines his
discussions to spoken linguistic conventions, Derrida also
addresses the nature of convention in written discourse and
language as a whole. Derrida defines writing as the attempt to
communicate with a reader who is absent. This process of
communicating with those who are not present means that
written signs must be "iterable" or repeatable. That is, signs
must remain readable beyond the immediate contexts in which
they were produced and be repeatable in new contexts and for
new addressees. (Speech need not necessarily be iterable, because one can imagine a speech situation in which one invents
a sign that serves a single instance for a single addressee and is
never used again; whereas writing, because the addressee is not
present, must rely on a repeatable code, if, Derrida argues, it is
to be identified as writing.) Derrida, like Davidson, looks for
and finds no conventional feature of language that accounts for
its repeatability and concludes that there is an unbridgeable gap
between words and their meanings. Therefore, we must not
look to convention to understand how meaning is communicated. Derrida and Davidson agree

that an irreconcilable split exists between the sign or sentence and its effect in the world. Because of this split, what Davidson calls "the autonomy of meaning" and Derrida calls "displacement," we can never be certain that our hermeneutic strategy—our use of signs—corresponds to another's hermeneutic strategy. Of course, social conditioning, the sharing of certain common practices, helps narrow the split by supplying a heuristic starting place for interpretation; that is, in day-to-day communicative interaction we assume that our neighbors employ the same hermeneutic strategy that we do, although, of course, we may be wrong. ("Paralogic Hermeneutics" 28)

In other words, communication always involves an interpretive act that is not systematizable because no two communication situations are exactly the same and no two communicants will have exactly the same language knowledge.

Kent argues that these interpretive acts are paralogic in nature—that is, beyond codification or systematization—because each time the writer encounters a new situation, he or she must invent a hermeneutic strategy in an effort to predict what will work. Davidson explains:

It is always an open question how well the theory an interpreter brings to a linguistic encounter will cope. In practice an interpreter keeps the conversation going by adjusting his theory on the spot. The principles of such inventive accommodations are not themselves reducible to theory, involving as they do nothing less than all our skill at theory construction. (xix–xx)

Convention only makes the guessing more accurate but never ensures that any particular guess will be the correct one.

Kent is well aware of the ramifications for composition theory, especially for social constructionist theory, in claiming that communication is not convention–bound. If the communication of meaning cannot be understood to be based on convention, then "many of our most influential theories of discourse production and analysis can explain satisfactorily neither the nature of language nor how the effects of language are produced" ("Beyond System" 505).

In order to move composition scholarship beyond the process paradigm, Kent provides a devastating critique of social constructionist theories. As Kent writes, the social constructionist approach

> assumes that a conventional link exists among the members of different discourse communities, and meaning as well as knowledge are grounded in socially constructed conventions; therefore, the sign (or the sentence) may be interpreted only through the sign's conventional effect in these different discourse communities. ("Beyond System" 504)

Kent questions not only the necessity of a foundational notion of the conventionality of language but also the usefulness of the concept of "discourse community"—a notion central to social constructionist theory.

Kent believes that the social constructionist concept of discourse community tells us very little about how meaning is communicated by discourse. He demonstrates first that social constructionists' views of discourse communities fall along a spectrum. At one end is the "thick" version of discourse community, in which such communities are represented as entities that can be identified and codified; they are envisioned as determinate systems that constitute frameworks from which the members of these communities understand the world. On the other end, other theorists endorse a "thin" version in which discourse communities are "a relatively indeterminate and uncodifiable sedimentation of beliefs and desires" ("Discourse Community" 425). The thin version understands discourse communities to be more fluid, more a "chorus of polyphonous voices," and one belongs to numerous and overlapping discourse communities simultaneously.

In his critique of common conceptions of discourse communities, Kent argues that such communities constitute what Davidson calls conceptual schemes—"ways of organizing experience; they are systems of categories that give form to the data of sensation; they are points of view from which individuals, cultures, or periods survey the passing scene" (Davidson 183).

In social constructionism a discourse community functions in much the same way as a conceptual scheme. As Kent explains:

> In the thick formulation, the social conventions that create the communities in which we live also constitute the framework we employ in order to survey the passing scene. In the thin formulation, we may survey the passing scene only by listening to and joining in the different and often contradictory voices that make up what Bakhtin calls the heteroglossia of community life. In both cases, however, our knowledge of others and of the world always will be relative to the particular conceptual schemes or communities in which we exist. (426)

Kent claims that rhetoricians can abandon the notion of discourse community because it does not tell us very much about the nature of discourse production other than that it is produced in social settings. In addition, the concept does not make logical sense:

> If members of different discourse communities speak, as Bruffee says, "quite different languages," then we could never understand them at all. Discourse communities cannot be incommensurate, for if they were, we would not even recognize them as being discourse communities. Therefore, the thick formulation of incommensurate discourse communities makes no sense. Of course, the thin formulation of commensurate discourse communities make no sense either, for if each discourse community is commensurate with every other one, we no longer need the concept of discourse community. (428)

Although Kent could be accused in this instance of drawing his categories rather too strictly in order to make his point, he is right in that the concept of discourse community offers little in the way of helping compositionists understand the nature of communicating meaning in social settings.

The problem can be avoided completely if, as Davidson advises, we abandon the Cartesian epistemological dualism that posits an "inside" and "outside": a separation between inside the subjective mind of the writer and outside in the objective world. As Kent writes:

> By claiming that our knowledge of the world is relative to a conceptual scheme, social constructionists endorse the Cartesian notion that a split exists between an "in here"— usually thought of as *mind* or *subjectivity*—and an "out there"—usually thought of as *world* or *objectivity*—a split that is mediated by a network of social conventions,

mental categories, or simply loosely-held beliefs. ("Discourse Community" 426)

Once composition theorists abandon the dualism of inside and outside—or, as Kent says, once they become "externalists" rather than "internalists"—they do not need the network of social conventions to connect the minds of writers with the world out there. Without the internal/external dualism, communication can be understood to take place between individuals unmediated by a discourse community or any other conceptual scheme. Thus, he argues that "we might better conceive of writing as a hermeneutic act that brings us in unmediated touch with the world and with the minds of others" (427).

In place of social constructionism and its reliance on Cartesian epistemology, Kent, as I said earlier, would have compositionists adopt an alternative view he calls "externalism." An externalist view holds "that propositional attitudes—our beliefs, intentions, desires, and so forth—derive from our public interactions with other language users and with the world. Consequently, mental states cannot exist without an external world" (430). Kent attempts to introduce compositionists to Davidson's "externalist" theory of communicative interaction, because Davidson has derived a communication theory that does not need to posit a conceptual scheme in order to account for the communication of meaning. According to Davidson, "communicative interaction" is necessary if meaning is to be communicated. This interaction takes place in a process he calls "triangulation." It takes place among three entities: "someone who thinks, other sentient beings, and a world they know and share" (430–31). In short, meaning is communicated directly by a process in which at least two individuals with some social connection engage in a dialogue that reveals to each what is commonly known about the nature of the world. These three positions occupy three apices of a triangle and are conceived of as a unity—if one has knowledge of one of the elements one *necessarily* has knowledge of the other two.

Unlike epistemological theories that currently underlie composition theory, Kent, via Davidson, provides a theory of discourse production and analysis that is more deeply enmeshed in social interaction, and hence in dialogism, than even social constructionist theories (with the possible exception of Freirean theory,[3] which is not strictly a composition theory but a literacy theory and which is not typically considered social constructionist):

> For a theory of discourse production, the consequence of Davidson's conception of triangulation concerns the light it throws on the social and public nature of communicative interaction.... From a Davidsonian perspective, writing becomes simply another species of communicative interaction that requires us to interpret continually and publicly the languages of others in an attempt to match our vocabularies with theirs. ("Externalism" 66–67)

In short, in order for meaning to be communicated, two people must engage in dialogue about objects in the world. In that process, knowledge about all three is revealed: the first speaker comes to know his or her own knowledge, something about the knowledge of the second person, and something about the object in question; the same is true reciprocally for the second person. According to Davidson, it is in the process of communicative interaction that concepts, beliefs, and knowledge come into existence. We know what we know, in other words, through dialogue. According to Kent, "To know that we intend or believe something can only mean that someone else will be able to interpret our belief or intention, and that our intention or belief refers to a world we share with others" ("Discourse Community" 431).

Because, in this scheme, there is no necessary foundation outside the dialogue that communicants "hook on to" in order to establish meaning, communicants are establishing meaning between themselves as the dialogue proceeds. In order to do this, they must share *some* amount of knowledge about language and the world, and, obviously, the more they share the more effective the communication. However, no communicant can know *in advance* of the dialogic situation how much he or she has in common with those he or she wishes to communicate with. Consequently, according to Davidson, communicants accept the fact that they "cannot be completely wrong about the beliefs and intentions of others" and operate on what he calls the "principle of charity," which constitutes the "opening move" in communicative interaction. It signals not only what vocabulary we desire to employ to talk about the world but also the assumption that others desire, at least initially, to believe our utterances ("Externalism" 64–65).

According to Davidson and Kent, although triangulation is a necessary condition for communicative interaction, it is not a wholly sufficient condition. When we triangulate we also must be able to interpret, on the run, the utterances of others. In order to do this, we are always engaged in what Kent calls hermeneutic guessing and what Davidson calls forming passing theories. Kent writes:

> For Davidson, communicative interaction requires on the spot interpretation that cannot be reduced to a schematic cognitive process or to any kind of epistemological system. As we communicate, we formulate

passing theories—tenuous strategies for understanding
the utterances of others—that cannot be formulated in
advance of a communicative situation. Consequently, a
passing theory should not be confused with something
like linguistic competence, for no framework—something
like a Chomskian grammar—established prior to
communicative interaction can explain what happens
during the act of communicative interaction.
("Externalism" 67)

In short, passing theories or hermeneutic guesses do not
substitute for any sort of *a priori* foundation that reliably
predicts how an utterance will be received. Passing
theories are generated "on the spot" and are specific to individual
communicative occasions.

Clearly, notions of communicative interaction and triangulation would move composition theorists' focus away from
internal mental constructs and cognitive processes and toward
a focus on interpretation and a public and dialogic concept of
discourse production. In fact, Kent understands the process of
producing and analyzing discourse as an intimate linking of
dialogue and interpretation—what he calls "dialogic interpretation"

where "dialogic" means an open-ended, non-systematic,
paralogic interaction between hermeneutic strategies.
Whenever we produce or analyze discourse, we always
guess at the hermeneutic strategy employed by someone
else, and when we guess, we engage the other in a kind of
dialogue in the sense that we continually interpret the
other's language code. This dialogue, in turn, always
brings about a tentative resolution of "meaning" that each
participant takes away from a communicative interchange,

and the tentative resolution enables the participant to enter new dialogic relations that consequently engender different effects in the world. When language codes intersect—when people converse together or a reader reads a text—resolutions are always generated, and these resolutions may or may not correspond precisely to a speaker's or writer's intention. If it corresponds precisely to anything, the resolution corresponds to the interpreter's sense of the ending resulting from a specific dialogic interaction; but it is important to note that this correspondence never results in closure, for the end of one dialogue simply signals the beginning of another. The conception of open-ended dialogue may be employed, I believe, to describe the paralogic/hermeneutic act intrinsic to both discourse production and analysis. ("Paralogic Hermeneutics" 31)

In other words, the process of dialogue—one that involves participants in constant interpretive guesses causing "on the spot" adjustments in the give-and-take of the dialogue—fundamentally describes speaking, writing, and reading. And this dialogic process is never ending: one dialogue ends in only a provisional settlement that in turn initiates another dialogue, and so on.

Thus, reading and writing are, in Kent's theory, fundamentally *processes*; however, they are not codifiable processes that can be reduced to linear steps, or even recursive steps like inventing, arranging, drafting, revising, and editing. Although those activities may occur, they do not account for how written and spoken discourse communicate meaning. It is only through our repeated attempts to communicate meaning to others and with others that we learn how to engage in dialogic interpretation or hermeneutic guessing. As Kent writes,

"Through our dialogic guessing, we learn what it takes to get things done in the world" (32).

This theoretical framework leads back to the question Kent raises: If reading and writing cannot be reduced to a codifiable system that predicts discourse activities with any certainty, how can these activities be described and how can they be taught? Even Kent admits that formal elements of discourse can be taught:

> Certainly, we can employ a metalanguage to teach variable elements of discourse such as grammar, punctuation, sentence construction, paragraph cohesion, expository modes, and the different generic conventions of academic essays, business letters, research reports, proposals, and so forth. Learning these elements, however, does not ensure in any way that a student can produce effective discourse. ("Paralogic Hermeneutics" 35–36)

In short, compositionists are in no way guaranteeing that a student can produce effective discourse when they teach the conventions of discourse or prescribed forms. In doing so, instructors are not ensuring that students can engage effectively in communicative interaction.[4] Effective communication emerges from the activity of interactive dialogue.

Toward a Paralogic Pedagogy

Kent has only sketched in broadest terms what a pedagogy based on his theory would entail. First, as I said earlier, part of Kent's program is to move composition beyond the process paradigm. When compositionists adopt an externalist view and refrain from talking about totalizing concepts of writing and, instead, understand writing as a fundamental species of dialogue, classroom focus on the process of writing can no longer be the primary focus of composition courses. According to Kent, process–oriented vocabularies can be dropped in favor of discussion of "concrete social and public uses of language" ("Externalism" 70). The primary focus could become producing written composition in specific situations and for specific audiences of concrete knowable others. Kent envisions a classroom in which students enter "into specific dialogic and therefore hermeneutic situations with others' interpretive strategies" ("Paralogic Hermeneutics" 37). In short, the classroom would be structured so that students can engage directly in communicative interaction or, in Ulmer's terms, the classroom would enact the scene of writing.

Consequently, Kent claims, the instructor in such a classroom "must relinquish the traditional role of lawgiver and assume the very different role of collaborator." The instructor becomes just one more voice in the dialogue, an advisor who "offers possible choices a student might make in her [or his] hermeneutic guessing about how to create effects in the world" (37).

Also, Kent maintains that composition instructors must realize the difference between monologic and dialogic writing: "Dialogic writing and reading occur when the student enters into collaborative—and therefore hermeneutic—interactions with the other; monologic writing and reading occur when the student cannot identify the other and, consequently, cannot converse with the other" (37). Much of the writing assigned in school is monologic; it tests memory or analytic skill or provides a basis for assigning grades. Monologic writing "does not allow dialogic/collaborative interaction between writer and reader; the student produces discourse that is essentially meaningless in the sense that no other responds to it, except perhaps the instructor who grades the discourse but never truly responds to it" (38). Dialogic writing would be understood as a response—already part of a communicative interaction, in which the student is attempting to communicate meaning to an other via the process of triangulation discussed above.

In an analysis of Kent's work, Raul Sanchez envisions further implications of Kent's theory, suggesting that an emphasis on individualized instruction best accomplishes students' engagement in communicative interaction:

> Since issues such as form, structure, organization, and the like are now incorporated into a consideration of more immediate contextual exigencies, the need for lectures or the traditional, teacher–lead class discussion is significantly reduced. Time might be better spent focusing on individuals' or small groups' particular problems, worries, and concerns as they work their way through specific discursive situations. (25)

Further, he argues that all writing that does not directly relate to the student's own engagement in communicative interaction becomes superfluous: "Because the 'content' of the course can at best be described as 'discourse,' the more time a student spends on producing and analyzing it the better" (25).

Referring to Ulmer's theatrical metaphors, we can say that the "scene of writing" in Kent's pedagogy would be a place where students engage in communicative interaction, where they perform or actually engage in "on the spot" dialogic interpretation in order to communicate meaning to an other who in turn responds, keeping the dialogue and the process of inquiry and knowlege–making moving along. In short, the classroom scene would be a performance of dialogic interaction. Students would write public discourse intended to get things done in the world rather than discourse thought of as practice. The goal of this kind of pedagogical method would be similar to that of radical pedagogy discussed in chapter three. The discourse must be produced with the goal of eventually having an effect in the world. In this public, dialogic interaction, writers would learn about themselves, others, and concrete reality.

Kent's applications of postmodern language theories of communication and language offer a comprehensive, intelligible, and useful employment of postmodern thought and dialogism to composition theory. Although much of Kent's theory reacts against the theoretical assumptions of social constructionist composition theory, in many ways he further refines composition studies' attempt to understand writing as a social and, hence, dialogic activity. Kent offers an alternative and more useful understanding of what is entailed when one uses written discourse in an effort to affect the world.

Postmodern Pedagogy and Dialogism

As Ulmer claims, a postmodern pedagogy is an inventive pedagogy, always involved in a process of seeking the available means by which we come to know. It assumes that knowledge unfolds in a dialogic interaction—a performance compared to a real life drama. Because knowledge is made evident in this dialogic process, all participants in the scene of teaching must be free to be inventive, free to enter into the dialogue. All participants must have speaking parts. Hence, the power to speak and invent must not be the teacher's alone but must be shared with the students. In a postmodern pedagogy, language does not stand between knowers and knowledge but is considered as constitutive of knowledge; language and knowledge are not separable terms. Situationality—that is, an emphasis on the specific social and public contexts within which discourse is produced and taught—is another primary focus, one that is especially important to the development of a postmodern pedagogy as well as a dialogic methodology. In addition, a postmodern dialogic pedagogy includes an investigation of the ways that power and values are implicated in truth claims and in the production of discourse; consequently, it will also include a self-reflective practice that makes part of its agenda a constant reexamination of its own claims to truth as well as its own motives, modes of operation, assumptions, and agendas.

Dialogic interaction cannot be achieved in authoritative, hierarchical situations that refuse some participants the power to speak and, thus, the opportunity to join in making knowledge or, as Freire would say, to join in the naming. Like liberatory learning advocates, theorists operating from a postmodern perspective understand that traditional "Hegelian" or "banking" pedagogies are based on epistemological assumptions that are at best outdated and, at worst, oppressive. Like radical pedagogy, postmodern pedagogy assumes that differences between "real" life, or everyday life, and pedagogy must be bridged if pedagogy is to have any significance. Also, both perspectives claim that learning is contextual. Dialogic instruction fosters learning by allowing the student to interact with others and the world, situating the student to pursue actively the unfolding of his or her own text through talking and responding to others. Learning to write, because writing is always simultaneously in response to and directed to another, is always a dialogic activity.

Covino attempts to devise a pedagogy that enacts the dialogic aspect of postmodern epistemology. He understands knowledge as an open-ended process that only attains provisional closure and always involves many voices and points of view. Thus, he proposes that students produce forms of discourse whose rhetorical purpose is to keep dialogue alive.

Unfortunately, he does not go far enough in formulating a pedagogy that performs open–ended dialogue. His methodology falls short because students' writing is never directed toward actual others who possess the ability to respond; the writing that Covino requires remains audienceless, arhetorical, and monologic "school discourse" that has little relation to the student or the instructor.

Like Covino, Kent fully understands the importance of dialogue for composition theory. Dialogue becomes an epistemological concept that describes how we come to know anything, including ourselves. It is in the process of attempting to communicate meaning—that is, the process of making a hermeneutic guess about what someone else will understand—that we come to know what we ourselves understand. As I have said before, knowledge unfolds in the process of dialogic, or communicative interaction. For years, compositionists such as Janet Emig have asserted that writing is intimately related to learning; now, Kent provides a theoretical construct that helps explain how this is so.

Dialogism, at least Kent's version, radically reframes composition studies. For instance, since language is not anchored in any system or conceptual scheme (such as internal mental structures) to give it meaning, we no longer need Elbow's concepts of private writing and nonaudience. All writing involves dialogue, involves some concept of audience—an internalized other to whom we write in order to understand ourselves. Elbow's concern that students will not learn how to be self–reflective with a concept of "nonaudience" proves unfounded. Indeed, Kent's theory argues that students become self–aware or self–reflective by engaging in dialogue, as Elbow's own insistence that young writers need immediate feedback implies. Postmodern theory such as Kent's dissolves expressivism's uneasy tension between the sovereign, interior world of the solitary writer and the necessity of interactive feedback with others.

In addition, postmodern pedagogy demonstrates how composition studies can leave behind the Cartesian subject/object dichotomy. Once the Cartesian dichotomy is successfully abandoned, communication can be understood as an unmediated process in which knowledge unfolds in a *dialogic interaction* that is situational or contextual and entirely public, having no anchor in a "reality" outside that dialogic interaction. And this, it seems, places composition and rhetoric at the epistemologic center of all learning:

> When we view writing and reading as paralogic/ hermeneutic acts, we come to see that writing and reading instruction resides at the very center of every student's academic curriculum, and when writing and reading become an integral part of every student's curriculum, the student will learn the important lesson that the creation and dissemination of knowledge takes place only within the discourses of social life and, in addition, the university may relearn that the production and analysis of discourse constitute the *raison d'être* of every academic discipline. ("Paralogic Hermeneutics" 39–40)

In short, if we agree with Kent, Davidson, and other postmodern theorists, then writing courses can no longer be conceived as "service" courses in which students learn standard forms of conventional discourse. The writing course becomes a site where students not only learn the metalanguage of composition, but, more importantly, also learn how to learn, how to "make knowledge."

However, there are some problems still to be solved in Kent's work and in postmodern theory in general. For instance, Kent's theory, as yet, focuses too much on speaking situations and has not sufficiently taken into account differences in the writer's situation. In speaking situations, it is easy to demonstrate how speakers make on the spot guesses about others' language codes. However, in composing written discourse the immediate audience, those interested in response, are often people that the writer never meets face-to-face. Immediate response is deferred into the future, and we have the problem that Derrida describes as writing to those who are absent. Can concepts of an internalized audience fully describe this situation? For instance, certainly, we can agree with Kent that a conceptual scheme like "discourse community" cannot provide a foolproof predictor of what will eventually be considered effective discourse by those who read it; however, before composition theory abandons the concept, perhaps we still need further investigation as to what ways it functions as an aid in the conventional choices that writers make. Perhaps discourse community could be conceived as the interaction of individual writers with the extant literature in particular fields. In this way, discourse communities are not conceived as groups of "foreign language" speakers, as in Bruffee, but as those who interact with a number of texts. It seems that some concept like discourse community remains useful to an understanding of how discourse has effects in the world.

Moreover, just as all the other perspectives discussed so far assume that dialogic pedagogy is democratic—that is, that there must be reciprocal trust and respect among conversants if all are to participate equally and honestly—postmodern composition pedagogy also claims awareness of the fact that uneven power relationships affect classroom settings. Unfortunately, however, postmodern theory remains blind to issues of individual difference (such as race, class, gender, and so on) that privilege the voices of some participants and silence others, a situation caused by uneven distribution of power in dialogic situations. This is most evident in Kent's reliance on Davidson's "principle of charity," which underlies communication interaction. The principle of charity allows a speaker to assume that he or she has enough in common with a potential respondent to initiate a dialogue and that the respondent will at least initially assume that the speaker is articulating what he or she believes to be true. As the work of Evelyn Ashton-Jones argues, in some communicative situations it is Davidson's principle of charity that is missing, especially in conversation among mixed gender groups. One could easily argue that many other types of inequities exist in dialogic situations. Yet, postmodern composition theorists have remained silent on these issues.

Clearly, application of postmodern theory will continue to revolutionize composition studies' notion of language and the underlying epistemological assumptions now largely taken for granted, and it represents the current frontier of composition scholarship. Like the other perspectives discussed, it provides some useful and some not so useful concepts of dialogism for composition studies. Perhaps, then, it is time that a new synthesis of current conceptions of dialogism in composition is attempted. The next chapter will attempt such a synthesis.

Notes

1. See Crowley's discussion in *A Teacher's Introduction to Deconstruction* (33–34) of Gayatri Spivak's review of Derrida's *The Post Card*.

2. See Ulmer's *Telethory*.

3. The similarities and differences between Freire's move away from Cartesian epistemology and that of Kent and Davidson will be discussed in chapter five.

4. This argument parallels the one that posits that knowing the rules of traditional grammar does not guarantee that students produce good writing and that direct instruction in such matters wastes valuable time that students should spend producing written documents. See Hartwell.

Toward a Functional Dialogism for Composition

> I felt discomfort lecturing to large numbers of students who I did not think needed to listen to me talk for fourteen hours each semester without "equal time" to answer, to talk back. I was bored and impatient in class because I was no longer participating in conversations, and I was teaching young people not to participate either. ... I became embarrassed that the young women in my classes waited to speak while the young men spoke out and got recognized by me immediately. I became convinced that my own classrooms were moments when students were taught to suppress their language, and where the language habits of sexism and racism were actually promoted.
>
> —Bleich, *The Double Perspective*

All of the compositionists I have discussed agree that learning takes place best through an interactive, dialogic process. A dialogic learning process seems especially suited to instruction in composition because of the dialogic nature of communicative processes themselves—that is, in the dialogic writing classroom, the activity to be learned is nearly identical to the process of learning it. However, as I demonstrated in the last four chapters, dialogic pedagogies employ differing and often conflicting ideological frameworks. Hence, they use dialogue in the writing classroom in different ways and try to achieve different, sometimes competing goals. This chapter attempts to synthesize the various uses of dialogism and to provide some additional methodological and theoretical frames in order to develop a functional dialogism for composition studies.

Because learning takes place best in communicative interaction, a functional dialogic pedagogy will have to employ a great deal of public writing—that is, writing directed to others capable of and interested in responding—if we are to produce students who are able to generate not only correct, readable prose, but also prose that can elicite a response from others, thereby enabling students to become active participants in communities beyond the classroom.

Each of the perspectives discussed in chapters one through four contributes something to a revised, functional view of dialogism for composition. In the following section, I will discuss how each perspective contributes to a functional synthesis of dialogism for composition studies. Then, I will discuss additional aspects necessary to make the concept of dialogism complete, ending with a more comprehensive view of dialogism and its implications for use in composition pedagogy.

Fundamental to a synthetic theory and practice of dialogism for the composition classroom is the concept of communicative interaction and hermeneutic guessing. Communicative interaction describes not only the process by which meaning is communicated in discourse but also the way any learning takes place. In this way, the learning process reproduces the goal of written discourse, which is the communication of meaning. From communicative interaction, all the competing dialogic practices or interactions fan out in many possible combinations. Thus, in talking about any particular aspect of a functional dialogism, often I will not be able to avoid talking about other dialogic relations as well. Nevertheless, so far, these dialogic interactions are distinguishable, if artificially so, as five principal types:

- internal dialogues between a self and an internalized audience

- dialogue between teacher and student

- dialogue between students and other larger social institutions, including but not limited to the educational institution or some other social institution within any one or more of the student's immediate communities

- dialogues among students about the formal matters of the composition or about the ideas or subject of the discourse

- composing using dialogic forms in order to understand an issue or group of issues from various points of view and gain insight into one's relationship to those ideas and into multiple perspectives represented by many voices that have already entered into public dialogue.

These types of dialogic interaction, however, do not represent a complete picture of the kind of functional dialogism I envision. We also need to consider other aspects of the social settings that make up college–level classrooms that can work to inhibit effective dialogue. Since all of the cited compositionists agree that truly democratic dialogue takes place only in an atmosphere of trust and mutual respect, it becomes crucial that participants have equal opportunity to engage in dialogue and that when they do participate that others truly listen and attempt to understand. Every student must view every other student as someone who has something valuable to contribute if dialogic situations are to function as optimal learning experiences. However, the unequal status of members within society as a whole reproduces itself in the classroom; students arrive in the classroom already in positions of unequal status, often unaware of the ways that differences in status affect their social interactions and often believing in the myth that classrooms are neutral spaces where gender, class, race, religion, occupation, and so on disappear. The latter half of this chapter will address this issue and methods that can be employed to develop the necessary trust for dialogue to function effectively.

Internal Dialogue: The Unfolding of Self-Knowledge

The expressivists largely see the production of written discourse as a one-way, solitary, and internal process involving a single author's attempts to communicate, yet they recommend that authors engage in various kinds of dialogic interaction with others during the process of producing a text. As discussed in chapter one, the primary goal of this pedagogy is self-discovery rather than communication with others, which is deemed a lesser goal.

Nevertheless, what expressivists, Elbow and Murray especially, offer to a functional dialogism is the beginning of a workable concept of internal dialogics. The goal of a revised internal dialogics would remain self-knowledge; however, the source of that knowledge shifts from an eternal and essential inner being struggling with an unwieldy and deceptive language in order to be heard to an internalized dialogue among internalized others.[1] The self in a dialogic pedagogy is not autonomous and solitary but multiple, composed of all the voices or texts one has ever heard or read and therefore capable of playing an infinite number of roles in service of the internal dialogic interaction. When writers' internal audiences obstruct or stifle them, they should be encouraged to imagine an internal audience that is anxious to engage in the dialogue at hand. Returning to Elbow's terms, students learn how to negotiate and manipulate their particular internal "dangerous" and "safe" audiences in productive ways in order to foster the continuation of internal dialogue that allows knowledge to unfold—just as in communicative interaction between two or more persons—in this case, the unfolding of self–knowledge.

Murray's concept of the writer's other self is one of these internal audiences, a rather specialized one who measures the possibilities for discourse against the necessity of a particular rhetorical situation. This is the internal audience who knows *how to*, who has gained experience with written discourse and understands the conventions of standard grammar and usage, who decides when to employ formal diction and when slang, who knows when the writing is going well and when not, who knows when to look for a more productive internal audience concept, and so on.

Elbow expresses concern in "Closing My Eyes As I Speak" that there is too much emphasis in composition pedagogy on the demands of external audiences, arguing that such emphasis cuts the student off from developing strategies of self–reflection in the absence of actual conversation. In a revised dialogic pedagogy, concepts of internal dialogue provide a balance to a pedagogy whose primary focus is communication of meaning to others capable of response, or public discourse. By providing students with the opportunity to develop conscious strategies for manipulating internal dialogue, composition instructors help each student understand his or her situation in relation to knowledge and to others. In other words, students come to understand that they also have a reciprocally dialogic relationship with knowledge. Here is a situation where various types of dialogues intermingle so as to be unable to distinguish separate voices and separate interactions involved— a place where one dialogue involves another. In order to explain this particular productive dialogic intermingling, I employ Don Bialostosky's application of some of Mikhail Bakhtin's theories to composition theory and pedagogy.

Internal Dialogic and "Ideological Becoming"

Bialostosky draws on dialogic concepts of discourse developed by Russian linguist and literary theorist Mikhail Bakhtin. Bialostosky argues that writing courses, especially those whose goal is to teach the conventions of academic discourse, tend to mask the dialogic nature of discourse. It is part of the convention of academic discourse to conceal "what Bakhtin calls the dialogizing background" (11). By covering the signs of dialogue, academic discourse presents arguments "as unified and the self that underwrites [them] as of one mind about it" and "enhances the appearance of authoritativeness and hides the possibility that the author did or could think otherwise" (11). This is the kind of discourse that Covino would call monologic, because it presents a picture of the author and the world as stable and unified.

Bialostosky is concerned that the emphasis on such conventions in writing courses leads students merely to learn forms without understanding how other voices (represented in other texts dealing with a subject) and intended audiences shape any particular discourse. He writes, "It is not enough, it seems, to learn to mind our academic manners, for we can still make fools of ourselves by not knowing to whom or after whom we are speaking" or writing (14). It is not enough, in other words, to write correctly; one must also understand how one's own knowledge is situated in relation to others' knowledge. Bialostosky addresses this issue via the theories of Bakhtin, who envisions the process of coming to know one's knowledge situation as a dialogic interrelationship of authoritative and internally persuasive discourse.

Authoritative discourse, which could also be called monologic discourse,

> can be received and repeated but is not to be responded to, modified, or questioned. It is the voice of the textbook or the lecturer that students learn to parrot back on tests, the voice of the instructor's summary judgment, the voice of given rules and conventions that must be observed but that do not have to account for themselves. (15)

It is also the voice of Freire's "banking" education and Ulmer's Hegelian education. It is a voice that is characterized as distant from and alien to students. Internally persuasive discourse forms a voice that exists within the student's "zone of contact." It is not the voice of the expressivists' autonomous, and solitary author; it is not the internal complement to authoritative discourse. On the contrary, it retains contact with both the individual and the social setting. Bakhtin writes:

> The internally persuasive word is half–ours, and half–someone else's. Its creativity and productivity consist precisely in the fact that such a word awakens new and independent words, that it organizes masses of our words from within, and does not remain in an isolated and static condition. It is not so much interpreted by us as it is further, that is, freely, developed, applied to new material, new conditions; it enters into interanimating relationships with new contexts. ("Dialogic Imagination" 345–46)

Internally persuasive discourse is conceived by Bakhtin as a discourse that is received, transformed, and then used. It arrives at the site of discourse production already laden with the meanings of others, and it "enters into an intense interaction, a *struggle* with other internally persuasive discourses" (346) and is transformed, developed, and applied to new situations and, in the process, becomes laden with additional or transformed meaning from an individual language user. Internally persuasive discourse represents dialogic knowledge in that it engages users in a struggle to understand its relationship to the knowledge that the user already has.

This internal struggle with discourse that is partly someone else's and partly one's own is what Bakhtin calls "an individual's ideological becoming" (342) and is closely related to Freire's concept of conscientization, or one's becoming critically conscious. This dialogic process allows students insight into their relationship to extant knowledge communities, allows them to understand their own ideological situation. Bialostosky writes:

> To know our minds as the site of dialogue among languages is to discover both the relevance of other people's words to our predicaments and the relevance of our contributions to others with whom we share the world and the ongoing dialogue about it. It is to take up membership not just in the community defined by the authority of a given discipline or religion or class and its language but in the whole community where those languages are in contention within and among the voices of speakers for whom they are internally persuasive. (17)

Bakhtin's concept of ideological becoming supports and extends Elbow's pedagogical goal of distinguishing private writing in order to "teach that crucial cognitive capacity to engage in extended and productive thinking," that is, students' capacity to "talk reflectively to *themselves*" ("Closing My Eyes" 62). It extends the pedagogical goal of self-knowledge through private writing by understanding self-knowledge *not* as a totally personal possession of the individual but, rather, as the identification of the nature of one's particular dialogic relationship to others, to knowledge, and to the world. In "talking reflectively to themselves," students uncover their situation in relation to the world; they become, according to Bialostosky, "ideologically situated persons involved in struggles over the meanings of things and the ownership of words" (15).

He sees the writing classroom as "a space in which individual ideological development can become not just the accidental outcome of encounters with the disciplinary languages but the deliberate goal of a reflective practice," a situation in which instructors are "free to engage [students] in intellectual struggles from which they learn to hold their own, . . . not just behave themselves" (16). In short, the writing classroom, among other things, becomes the space where students learn how to engage in dialogue productively with themselves. Hence, a concept of internal dialogue becomes an integral component in a balanced, functional dialogic pedagogy.

Instructional methodologies that are already familiar to composition can be employed in the service of developing students' internal dialogue. For example, students can be asked to write synthesis journals in which they are asked to explain ideas presented in their reading to themselves in their own words—engaging in a dialogue with another's written text—making connections among ideas and relating them to what they already know and their everyday lives.[2] In journals or in more formal written assignments, students could construct dialogues in which they place themselves and their own points of view in dialogue with experts on a particular subject, much as Covino suggests. To extend the dialogue further, these dialogues could be shared with classmates, so students could also understand how other students in turn situate themselves in relation to knowledge, perhaps deepening their own understanding of their situation.

Dialogism and Peer Criticism

Another significant aspect of a revised dialogic pedagogy would be based on Bruffee's method of peer criticism (described in detail in chapter two), which combines dialogic interaction on several levels. Although internal dialogue is not abandoned, the focus of the dialogic interaction now is more clearly on communicating with concrete others, most notably classroom peers who one expects to respond and to whom one will respond. In peer criticism, several simultaneous dialogues occur: students compose documents directed as much as possible to a public audience about an issue with which they have some personal relationship; they talk together, as a class or in small groups, about various aspects of composing; and they compose several kinds of written responses to other students' compositions. Students engage most directly in communicative interaction with other students when speaking face–to–face about writing and ideas with other students and in the written responses to other students' compositions. It is in these encounters that students can most efficiently employ Kent's hermeneutic guessing strategies and where they can see almost immediately the results of their guesses. As I said in chapter two, from a rhetorical point of view, this pedagogy engages students in multiple and various rhetorical situations, allowing students a great deal of practice attempting to communicate meaning to others as well as providing a great deal of feedback.

I would further complicate the dialogic interactions of

Bruffee's pedagogy by asking that the actual essays (rather than the peer responses) that students' compose be addressed to audiences beyond the classroom and that students attempt to take part in the discourse of public life. Unfortunately, the writing assignments in Bruffee's *Short Course in Writing* are too often arhetorical writing exercises without specific purposes and public audiences. I understand that all writing assignments need not be addressed to audiences and purposes outside the classroom, but the majority should be so addressed. Otherwise, students engage in a form of dialogic interaction that is unnecessarily limited and in the long run has little transferability to other rhetorical situations.

This type of dialogue intermingles or overlaps with radical pedagogy's emphasis on the necessity that the ultimate goal of students' discourse and inquiry be the transformation of oppressive social situations. As you will remember from chapter three, Freirean *praxis* always involves reflection and action. One reflects on one's situation in order to name the situation with internally persuasive terms, thereby coming to understand critically one's relationship to power structures that include (but are not limited to) knowledge communities; educational institutions; socially constructed stereotypes of gender, racial, and class; and so on. Ultimately, critical reflection must result in some kind of action to transform oppressive social structures, and in literate societies these transformative actions involve the use of written discourse. Even if one finds this discussion about oppressive social structures rather extreme in reference to North American college composition classrooms, one cannot escape the fact that a great deal of the work" ofbusiness, government, education, religious institutions, and so on is accomplished through the dialogic interaction of written documents. Therefore, it seems crucial that much of the writing done in college–level composition classes address real audiences and concern situations that are of importance to the student and to his or her community.

The Role(s) of the Instructor in a Dialogic Writing Class

A common belief of the compositionists I have discussed is that the setting of the composition classroom cannot be one in which an expert lectures and novices passively listen. Elbow's teacherless class, Bruffee's peer criticism, liberatory learning theorists' radical classrooms, and poststructualists' postmodern classrooms that enact the scene of writing all reconstruct the composition classroom in dialogic ways. Authority and expertise are no longer assumed to be the sole province of the instructor. However, it is too simplistic to envision a classroom in which the roles are merely reversed. All authority is not surrendered to students, just as all authority cannot remain with the instructor.

There are various roles that a composition instructor can assume in the dialogic classroom: fellow writer, editor, coach, facilitator, good listener, orchestrator of beginnings but rarely controller of outcomes, and, finally, in many cases an evaluator and assigner of grades. Just as the focus of the dialogue shifts over time, so will the role of the instructor, often being determined by which aspect of the dialogue students are engaged in at any given moment.

As coach, an instructor can help students master the strategies for dealing with the mechanics of written discourse, showing them effective ways to increase their reading ability, for solving punctuation problems, or for solving any of the other formal problems that may arise in any particular student's engagement with the conventions of written discourse.

Many compositionists recommend that instructors either bring their current writing projects to class or participate with the students in the kinds of discourse that are part of the course. This strategy has the advantage of bringing the instructor into dialogue at a concrete level, making him or her directly part of the interaction. However, the danger is that the group will become dependent on the instructor's perceived "expertise," thus nullifying the contributions of the other members of the group.

Sometimes the instructor only needs to act as an encouraging other—that is, a facilitator or good listener—thereby validating students' experiences and aiding them in identifying the strategies that are working efficiently for them. This role is closest to Murray's notion of training the writer's "other self," discussed in chapter one.

Playing the role of editor is one that I have found productive in composition classroom. In the technical writing class, I assume the role of the owner of a firm that provides technical writers to other professional firms on a temporary as–needed basis; at other times, I have asked the students to assume this role. They or I then attempt to evaluate the effectiveness of finished technical documents before they are sent to our professional customers and before we bill them for our services. In expository writing classes, I ask students to write query letters—sometimes addressed to me as a fictional editor, sometimes to actual editors of national periodicals—explaining why a particular article they have written or would like to write is appropriate for that particular market. In order to do this, the students must solve different audience problems: first, the persuasive task of convincing an editor that their article is right for his or her magazine, and, second, the task of attempting to understand the demands of the audience of the national periodical.

Finally, there is the most difficult problem for a dialogic theory of learning: grades. In a dialogic classroom, authority is shared; however, eventually the instructor must use his or her authority—to satisfy institutional mandates—to make evaluative judgments about students, which is in many ways antithetical to the spirit of dialogue. The mandate that individual students be graded undermines dialogue and demonstrates how antithetical dialogic pedagogy is to the institutional setting in which I advocate its use. In a utopian university of the future where the dialogic spirit informs entire institutions of higher learning, one could envision abandoning practices that are so antithetical to that spirit. However, in a functional pedagogy devised to be useful today, the evaluative practice of assigning grades must remain in uneasy tension with the dialogic practices.

After I had given a presentation based on chapter three of this work to a group of professors, one asked me about a situation that he encounters in his teaching life: "What about when I have a group of students and I have all sorts of interesting and exciting stuff that I know and want to share with them about the life of D.H. Lawrence?" The question he was really asking is, "Is there never a time when it is appropriate to lecture?" I would say that yes, there will be times even in a dialogic classroom when lecturing might be appropriate. In the professor's situation, he could very well lecture, if it were clear that the direction of the dialogic inquiry led the group in that direction. He should also be prepared for a situation in which the students wish to use his expertise in Lawrence scholarship in other ways—for instance, in helping them understand the historical and cultural contexts in which Lawrence wrote, or a situation in which some of the students may indeed be interested in the biographical details of Lawrence's life, or Lawrence's contributions as a painter, and so on. In short, the progress of the inquiry in a dialogic classroom is not solely controlled by the instructor.

Ideally, the dialogic classroom constructs the subject of class inquiry through dialogic interaction of the expertise of the instructor and the particular needs and interests of a particular group of students. As Freire says in a recent interview:

Dialogue and respect for students and their contexts do not mean that the teacher has to disappear or, in other words, that the teacher does not have to teach. It's impossible for me to imagine the existence of a teacher without teaching. That is, the teacher has the duty to teach. The question for me is how the teacher uses his or her authority. I'm not against the authority of teachers. I am against the hypertrophy of authority against the fragility of students' freedom, and I am against the hypertrophy of students' freedom against the fragility of authority. ("History, *Praxis*, and Change" 159–60)

In other words, a dialogic classroom is one in which the authority of instructor and student is always in a state of productive and balanced tension—a tension maintained by engagement in dialogue at every level of discourse.

Incorporating Conflict and Difference into Dialogism

Expressivist, social constructionist, and poststructuralist/postmodern dialogic theories tacitly assume that students are the same—or at least similar enough—thus enabling theorists to assume that differences among students will not affect the projected outcomes of pedagogical methodologies. Liberatory learning, although it recognizes that students are differentiated along class lines—oppressed and oppressor class—was largely developed in situations where the students (male peasants) shared a world outlook and a great deal of common experience. All of these theories are largely blind to differences such as gender, ethnicity, class (especially when class members come from various class strata), religion, or race. In fact, most mainstream theories still assume a "universal student" modeled on white, middle- to upper–class male students; yet, college classrooms increasingly reflect the diversity of U.S. contemporary culture. Moreover, as I discussed in chapter two, a number of social constructionist theorists argue that such interactive pedagogies foster democratic interaction and values, a claim I will demonstrate is simplistic.

In recognizing that there are various ways that dialogue enables writers to improve, as I have already argued, it becomes necessary then to ensure that the social setting of the classroom is such that all students actually engage in the various dialogues and that they feel comfortable enough to expose personal experiences, even when they experiences may conflict with the experience or attitudes of other members of the class. The compositionists discussed in this work agree that dialogic methods are best employed in an atmosphere of trust and mutual respect. However, all of these theorists fail to address possible ways that unequal social structures of classrooms inhibit this atmosphere. Because of the unequal status of students in many of our classrooms, a trusting atmosphere is often difficult to initiate and maintain.

A dialogic composition pedagogy still needs a way to accommodate differences among students. The next section addresses the issues of student difference and the unequal social relationships often involved in such difference and how it can affect productive dialogic interaction in negative ways. I will discuss, for the most part, differences in gender, but I understand that gender is but one of a cluster of differences among students including race, class, ethnicity, religion, sexual orientation, age, and so on.

Feminist Epistemology and the Accommodation
of Difference

There are a growing number of educators who are beginning to recognize and explore these issues. For example, Susan Jarratt, in a recently published article, expresses concern that dialogic pedagogies that place "a high priority on establishing a supportive and accepting climate" (105) run the risk of becoming oppressive because they suppress conflict caused by the uneven social positions among students and even between students and instructor. Jarratt, whose work I will return to in more detail later, writes, "Paradoxically, when groups do work together in these pedagogies, the ideal is homogeneity, another way of avoiding confrontations over social differences" (109). In short, Jarratt argues, similarly to Evelyn Ashton–Jones (see chapter two), that dialogic composition pedagogies have the same potential as any other composition pedagogies to reinforce racism, sexism, and classism (109). As Ashton–Jones persuasively argues, these pedagogies assume that

> those speaking from marginalized and "different" perspectives—be it from the perspective of race, ethnicity, gender, class, age, sexual orientation, or occupation—will, in fact, have access to the conversation and, further, that the dynamics of the conversation itself will remain unaffected by a given participant's "difference." (3)

Putting people in groups and asking them to engage in dialogue does not necessarily lead to situations in which students learn productively and does not necessarily reinforce democratic ideals.

Ironically, feminists have embraced forms of dialogic pedagogy as a subversion of patriarchal educational values such as competition and hierarchy. As Ashton–Jones points out,

"Feminist scholarship has been quite explicit and nearly unanimous in framing collaborative learning as a boon for women students, who have encountered sexism and male bias in more traditional pedagogies and who struggle with the androcentric perspectives that pervade the academy" (6). However, as both Ashton–Jones and Jarratt argue, feminists have perhaps too hastily embraced these pedagogies, and further examination of how they actually affect student interaction is necessary.

In a feminist critique of traditional Western epistemology, Lorraine Code provides insight both into why dialogic forms of inquiry are antithetical to traditional pedagogical methods and why women and other marginal groups have often found themselves in conflict with these methods. Code argues that although epistemology has claimed to be "neutral and universally objective" and therefore "explicitly gender–neutral," its appeal to neutrality "masks the facts of its derivation from and embeddedness in a specific set of interests: the interests of a privileged group of white men" (x). In other words, epistemology, rather than being neutral, is already invested in a value system that privileges traditional Western male values, values that have traditionally evaluated women in a negative light and have led to their social oppression. I argue that the same would be true of any pedagogy that is derived from such epistemology or that fails to articulate its difference from such gendered epistemological assumptions, including a dialogic pedagogy.

Like the pedagogical theorists I have discussed, traditional epistemologists presuppose an ideal Cartesian knower; that is, "all knowers are believed to be alike with respect both to their cognitive capacities and to their methods of achieving knowledge" (6). They understand inquiry as an "introspective activity of an individual mind" having no relevance to either "a knower's embodiment or his (or her) intersubjective relations" (5) and that knowledge is gained by reasoned thought, unassisted by the senses. They consider the question of who a knower might be inappropriate because it undermines any claims to objectivity and leaves epistemology hopelessly mired in relativity. Code, however, argues that traditional epistemologists, by failing to address the circumstances of the knower, provide only limited understanding of what it means to know anything. She argues that epistemologists must reconsider the role of such subjective factors as the gender of the knower if they are to claim to "tell the whole story" (4). She writes, "In proposing that the sex of the knower is epistemologically significant, I am claiming that the scope of epistemological inquiry has been too narrowly defined" (7).

Code views traditional epistemological thought as dominated by objectivity and demonstrates how the dominance of objectivity over subjectivity has affected the ways that concepts of male and female are understood:

The relation of the objective/subjective dichotomy to the male/female dichotomy is apparent from the fact that, in the philosophical tradition, women are often (albeit perhaps unthinkingly) consigned to an insignificant place in a community of knowers on the basis of claims that *their* "knowledge" is hopelessly subjective. Such claims are commonly based on women's purported incapacity to rise above the practical, sensuous, and emotional preoccupations of everyday life. Hence women are judged unfit for the abstract life of pure reason in which true knowers must engage. So a set of dichotomies continuous with the subjective/objective dichotomy is invoked: theory/practice, reason/emotion, universal/particular, mind/body, abstract/concrete. They demarcate a set of categories—the lefthand one of each pair—by which knowledge is distinguished from aspects of experience deemed too trivial, too particular, for epistemological notice. The alignment of the righthand terms of these pairs with (stereotypical) femininity is well established. (28–29)

From this and other such evidence, Code concludes that

The objective/subjective dichotomy occupies a central position in mainstream epistemology, marking off knowledge that is worthy of its title from less worthy contenders. The complex, gender specific workings of that dichotomy show without doubt that the sex of the knower *is* epistemologically significant. The veneration of ideal objectivity and the concomitant denigration of subjectivity are manifestations of a "sex/gender system" that structures all the other inequalities of western social arrangements and informs even those areas of life—such as "objective" knowledge—that might seem to be gender-free. (67)

Thus, it is naive for theorists of dialogic pedagogy to assume that social arrangements in composition classrooms and pedagogies derived from them will not be structured by these same sex/gender systems that structure such assumed value-neutral concepts as "objective knowledge."

Code also argues that women have a hard time establishing themselves as credible knowers because feminine stereotypes have constructed them negatively:

Like any other knower, a female knowledge claimant has to claim acknowledgment from other participants in a form of life. But advancing such claims is as much a political action as it is a straightforwardly epistemological one. Before she can so much as seek acknowledgment, a woman has to free herself from stereotyped conceptions of her "underclass" epistemic status, her cognitive incapacity, and her ever-threatening irrationality. She has to achieve this freedom both in the eyes of other people, who too often deny her capacity by refusing to listen or give credence, and from her own standpoint, shaped as it also is by stereotype-informed assumptions that neither her experiences nor her deliberative capacities are trustworthy sources of knowledge. (215)

A woman is in danger of not being viewed as credible by others; more importantly, however, sometimes she herself lacks confidence in her ability to act as "knowledge claimant." Especially now, when so many young women believe that gender issues are no longer important because they believe all the problems have already been solved, a woman may attribute the dismissal of her knowledge claim by others as an indication that her claim was invalid; she may not investigate the possibility that others' reaction is the result of stereotypic assumptions about her credibility. She may then drop lines of inquiry before they are fully developed, prematurely closing off communicative interaction. That women have a credibility problem is supported by the scholarship that Ashton–Jones cites. In conversational situations involving mixed-gender groups, topics introduced by women were more readily dropped by the conversants than those initiated by male group members. Clearly, a woman in such a position in a dialogic writing classroom is not fully participating in the kind of communicative interaction in which knowledge of herself, of others, and of the world unfolds; thus, there is the grave potential that she is disadvantaged rather than empowered in such dialogic situations.

This situation can be further complicated by feminist theories that, as Code writes, attempt to celebrate feminine knowledge by "evaluative reversals"—that is, by positing traditional representations of feminine values such as care, sensitivity, responsiveness and responsibility, intuition and trust in place of traditional masculine values of competition, individuality, objectivity, reason, skepticism, and so on. Yet, these same feminine values have become—at least for "women of prosperous classes and privileged races"—the distinctions that have kept women in positions of powerlessness and inferiority (17). Code reminds women who wish to celebrate an essential, eternal feminine ideal that "women are also represented, in essentialist thought, as naturally less intelligent, more dependent, less objective, more irrational, less competent, more scatterbrained than men" (18). Hence, there is a tension in feminist thought between wanting to celebrate those positive representations of the feminine and a "fear of endorsing those same values as instruments of women's continued oppression" (17).

The stereotypic set of values that some feminists wish to celebrate and which is reinforced by traditional epistemological categories can undermine women in dialogic situations in other subtle ways by putting them in a curious double bind. First, if they celebrate feminine values and ways of knowing, they risk losing credibility as objective thinkers, thus risk not being "taken seriously" by their audience; second, if they deny those same feminine values and represent themselves as objective thinkers, they lose association with valuable, positive feminine values—care, sensitivity, responsibility and responsiveness—the very attributes that would contribute to the development of a trusting atmosphere in a dialogic classroom. These same sex/gender dynamics can also work against a female instructor, undermining in either a subjective or objective direction her ability to foster productive, democratic, dialogic interaction.

> A female teacher who takes a position of uncritical openness toward the male student, especially if social–class differences also apply, invites the exercise of patriarchal domination to which every man in our society is acculturated. Because most high school teachers are women and may be seen as maternal figures, the role of supportive, nurturing composition teacher repeats that childish pattern and puts the teacher at a disadvantage in any attempt to assert a counterhegemonic authority as a women. (Jarratt 111)

How then is a woman to negotiate communicative interaction in such a way that it is productive for her own "ideological becoming" and without adopting the traditional patriarchal, monologic modes of discourse? I will answer this question so far as I can by drawing further on Jarratt's and Code's work and on a theory of communicative ethics recently proposed by Sharon Welch.

Reviewing the early work of feminist rhetoricians, Jarratt is also concerned that composition instructors influenced by expressivist pedagogies and feminist pedagogies that attempt to reverse patriarchal values suggest to students that cooperation, care, and nurturing involve not "stepping on anyone's toes." While she acknowledges the "note of hope" that these pedagogical theories provide, she argues that they still need more openly to acknowledge gender, race, and class differences among students.

> We must work to strengthen the goal of displacing teacher authority with a more carefully theorized understanding

of the multiple forms of power reproduced in the classroom. Differences of gender, race, and class among students and teachers provide situations in which conflict does arise, and we need more than ideal harmonious, nurturing composition classes in our repertory of teaching practices to deal with these problems. (113)

Hence, it becomes necessary that a functional dialogic pedagogy not only provide an atmosphere of mutual respect and trust but also that it acknowledge that in the process of dialogic interaction, conflicts among students or between students and an instructor may need to be negotiated because discursive practices cannot be separated from the people that engage in them and the social contexts that motivate them.

I would endorse Jarratt's vision of what such a classroom would be like:

My hopes are pinned on composition courses whose instructors help their students to locate personal experience in historical and social texts—courses that lead students to see how differences emerging from their texts and discussions have more to do with those contexts than they do with an essential and unarguable individuality. I envision a composition course in which students argue about the ethical implications of discourse on a wide range of subjects and, in so doing, come to identify their personal interests with others, understand those interests as implicated in a larger communal setting, and advance them in a public voice. (121)

Dialogue in Jarratt's composition classroom includes both the heat of argument as well as the warmth of a nurturing environment within which to engage in productive communicative interaction. If students are to participate in the kind of dialogic interaction that fosters what Bakhtin calls earlier in this chapter "ideological becoming," then they must also understand that other voices in the dialogue will at times conflict with theirs, that other students will make unwarranted assumptions about them and their lives (as they themselves will about others and their lives), and that what is most important is that the dialogue continue, that the participants continue to learn about themselves, about others, and about the world.

If dialogic classrooms are going to function as I have been describing, it is apparent that they also need a clear underlying epistemological and ethical framework. What must be avoided is the kind of relativistic pluralism in which all opinions are afforded equal weight by the group; as Code says, "Some knowledge claims are *better* than others" (4). Conversely, the forced imposition of knowledge claims by particular members of the class or by instructors must be avoided. The process of determining which knowledge claims are better than others is not a process that works from the top down, from positions of privilege and power to positions of powerlessness. As liberatory learning theorists claim, the process must involve dialogue between groups. Therefore, dialogic pedagogy needs to be informed by an epistemology that values more than objective knowledge and that recognizes that knowledge making is a collective endeavor. In addition, it needs an ethical framework that fosters and values a multiplicity of voices without invalidating differences among participants.

Code proposes a revision of traditional epistemology that balances subjective and objective knowledge claims. Traditional epistemology, modeled largely on the methodological and epistemological criteria of the science of physics, still assumes that what can be called knowledge is "value–neutral" and "that objects of knowledge are separate from knowers and investigators and that they remain separate and unchanged throughout investigative, information–gathering, and knowledge–constructing processes" (31–32). She acknowledges that few practicing scientists believe in such "perfect objectivity," yet mainstream epistemologists continue to construe knowledge in "these stringent objectivist terms" (32). She argues that this strict understanding of objectivity limits epistemologists' ability to describe knowledge in other than such strict scientific arenas such as the physical sciences. And, as I discussed earlier, Code demonstrates how the rigid objectivity of traditional epistemology has led to reinforcing the stereotype of women as inferior knowers because of their continued association with subjectivity. She writes:

> Constructing distinctions as polar opposites, conceiving their boundaries as fixed and rigid, and confining inquiry within the limits those boundaries impose are unduly restrictive of philosophical insight. When theorists use such dichotomies to mark distinctions that are both hierarchical and polar, they establish a set of exclusionary, oppressive constraints and imbalances. By contrast, the approach to knowledge I shall sketch highlights possibilities of reciprocal interaction between and among such constructs. (28)

Code argues that an epistemology that admits the interaction of subjectivity and objectivity is not hopelessly relativistic. Critics of relativism have argued that

> the only honest—and logical—move a relativist can make is once and for all to declare his or her skepticism. Where there are no universal standards, . . . there can be no knowledge worthy of the name . . . that relativism is

simply incoherent because of its inescapable self–referentiality. . . . In short, relativism is often perceived as a denial of the very possibility of epistemology. (2–3)

Code, in contrast, contends that relativism need not be understood in such extreme terms. She argues that there are advantages to understanding relativism as an enabling position rather than a constraining position. Relativism is one means of "avoiding reductive explanations, in terms of drastically simplified paradigms of knowledge, monolithic explanatory modes, or privileged, decontextualized positions."

For a relativist, who contends that there can be many valid ways of knowing any phenomenon, there is the possibility of taking several constructions, many perspectives into account. Hence relativism keeps open a range of interpretive possibilities. At the same time, because of the epistemic choices it affirms, it creates stringent accountability requirements of which knowers have to be cognizant. Thus it introduces a moral–political component to the heart of epistemological enquiry. (3)

Thus, according to Code, relativism allows knowers to make comparisons between competing knowledge claims, opens the possibility of knowing something in more than one way, and helps knowers avoid having to posit a single and unitary view of the world when they actually understand the world from a multiplicity of knowledge claims and points of view. Her position accords in many ways with Covino's discussed in chapter four.

One important form of subjective knowing that Code reclaims for epistemology is knowing other people, a form of knowing that is also important to a functional dialogic pedagogy. Code believes that "knowing other people" constitutes an additional paradigm of knowing that is different from and as important as knowing everyday objects:

> Knowledge of other people develops, operates, and is open to interpretation at different levels; it admits of degree in ways that knowing that the book is red [objective knowledge] does not. Hence it is qualitatively different from the simple observational knowledge commonly constitutive of epistemological paradigms. (37)

Code admits that the degree to which other people are knowable "may sit uneasily with psychoanalytic claims about the unconscious, and postmodern critiques of theories that presuppose a unified self" (37). However, she is not talking about knowing, in this situation, as it is understood within the confines of traditional, objectivist epistemology:

> Knowing other people, precisely because of the fluctuations and contradictions of subjectivity, is an *ongoing, communicative, interpretive process.* It can never be fixed or complete: any fixity that one might claim for "the self" is at best a fixity in flux; but something must be fixed to "contain" the flux even enough to permit references to and ongoing relationships with "this person." Assumptions that one knows another person have to be made within the terms of this tension. (38; emphasis added)

Thus, in providing students an epistemological framework that allows for the interaction of subjective and objective knowledge and an epistemological paradigm that validates knowing other people as part of a revised dialogic pedagogy, we are providing a vehicle in which students' lived experiences that designate their social differences find a place to surface, be heard, and enter into the communicative interaction from which they gain knowledge of themselves, of others, and of the world.

This position most closely resembles Freire's theoretical position, discussed in chapter three. Freire, as previously stated revises the dichotomy of subject/object into a unity that is understood in his concept of *praxis*. In order to learn effectively, groups of students reflect subjectively on their immediate situation in the concrete, objective world in order to transform those situations, always moving closer to situations that foster the humanity of oppressed and oppressor alike. Freire conceives subject/object as an inseparable unity: people with the world and the world with people. Kent's pedagogical theory (chapter four), in contrast, attempts to bypass the Cartesian dichotomy altogether by positing that people communicate directly with other people about the objective world; therefore, all communication is external, situated in the concrete world, and there is no need to bother with concepts of inside/outside, mind/body, subject/object, thought/speech, and so on.

I believe that the epistemological position that views subjectivity and objectivity in dialectical interaction, as in Freire and Code, is particularly useful for a functional theory of dialogic pedagogy because it allows individuals to understand that there is a personal, subjective aspect to their knowledge but that their personal knowledge is always relational to the knowledge of others and to so-called objective knowledge about the world. However, as Code writes, this view of epistemology, because it affords choices, "introduces a moral–political component into the heart of epistemological enquiry" and, I would argue, into the heart of dialogic pedagogy. Code's revision of traditional epistemology provides a way to theoretically understand the relationship and value of both subjective and objective knowledge to our classroom. However, it still leaves us with the problem of negotiating conflicts while, at the same time, fostering the kind of productive atmosphere in which true democratic dialogue can take place. What is needed is an ethical framework that allows multiple and conflicting issues to emerge without allowing any one point of view to dominate and close off continued dialogue.

Welch proposes such an ethical framework in the form of a *communicative ethics* that argues for the "ethical imperative of highlighting differences," an argument she does not see currently addressed in appeals to reason or in "the denial of grounded ethical and political critique by some postmodern theorists" (84). Welch argues that it is the "material interaction between multiple communities with divergent principles, norms, and mores [that] is essential for foundational moral critique," in contrast to communal theories that presuppose a cohesive community in which the members share principles, norms, and mores (86). The Aristotelian polis is often used as paradigmatic of the successful functioning of such communal ethics, and Welch argues that such a community lacks the means to criticize constitutive forms of injustice, forms of exclusion and limitation (like the Athenian institutions of slavery and the oppression of women) central to the operation of a given social system" (86–87). Moral critique can emerge only during certain kinds of material interaction—political conflict, coalition, or joint involvement in life-sustaining work—between communities with divergent values.

> What led to Aristotle's defence of slavery is what is most dangerous in our own society: the assumption that one's own community and social class possess the prerequisites for moral judgment and that other groups are devoid of those same prerequisites. . . . Aristotle dismisses

non–Greeks, barbarians, and slaves as "incapable" of political relationships, and thus incapable of participating in political forms which are necessary for the existence of virtue. (87–88)

Greek society was unable to challenge the ethical positions that led to the institution of slavery and the oppression of women because of the confidence in its own superiority that was based on "an ethic of exclusion" and isolation—in this case, the exclusion and isolation by privilege of all who were not "free men."

Communicative ethics, according to Welch, seeks to avoid the exclusion and isolation of privilege by understanding that *"foundational ethical critique requires difference"* (88). One can perceive foundational flaws in systems of ethics only from positions of difference, "from the perspective of another system of defining, and implementing, that which is valued. In order to determine which interests or positions are more just, what is required is pluralism, not for its own sake, for the sake of enlarging our moral vision" (88).

However, if ethical systems are to avoid devolving into systems of exclusion, then what is essential to communicative ethics is that the engagement in moral critique be reciprocal and mutual. Welch writes, for example, that

Euro–American feminists are justified in criticizing the oppression of women in other cultures, criticizing Indian suttee, for example, and African genital mutilation. We must remember, however, that critique goes both ways. Genuine communication has not occurred until we become aware of the flaws in our culture that appear quite clearly from the vantage point of Indian and African societies, . . . for example, an Indian critique of the Western treatment extreme individuality and valorization of symmetry and order. (88)

In short, communicative ethics demands that we encourage reciprocal critique among groups of people; discernment of foundational ethical defects requires the concrete interaction among communities. Communicative ethics hopes that when conflicts arise in the form of criticism that they can do so without dominating the class and curtailing the dialogue.

However, Welch argues that transformative dialogue—a dialogue in which both the more– and less–privileged participants are changed (something similar to Freirean dialogue)— "occurs only [in] the fruition of more fundamental interchanges" (97). In these interchanges, all participants demonstrate their solidarity as human beings. They come to see all participants as humans, or as Freire says, they all recapture the humanity that was wrested from them because of the unequal power relationships that create oppression in societies. In these fundamental interchanges, it is not necessary that we all agree about issues, but that in expressing solidarity all grant "each group sufficient respect to listen to their ideas and to be challenged by them, [and] recognition that the lives of the various groups are so intertwined that each is accountable to the other" (95). To the extent that participants engaged in dialogue are able to express such "solidarity in difference" is the extent to which dialogic interaction has the potential of becoming a truly liberating and transforming human experience for the participants.

Hence, an epistemological stance that validates subjective as well as objective knowledge and an ethical stance that allows conflict while it encourages the hearing and evaluation of many viewpoints and fosters solidarity among those engaged in dialogue is necessary for the successful functioning of dialogic pedagogies in college-level composition courses. Moreover, these notions of epistemology and communicative ethics have to become part of the dialogue of the classroom so that the injustices that they are designed to avoid are made visible and therefore available for transformation in the dialogic situation—so that students can understand when they are acting in ways that close off dialogue and, thus, curtail their and other learning opportunities.

Toward a Comprehensive Dialogism

As this work has demonstrated, compositionists are largely locked into a variety of ideological frames, and therefore their concepts of dialogic pedagogy are accordingly limited. I have attempted in this work to expand composition studies' notion of dialogue and its potential as an organizing concept in pedagogical theory and classroom practice. I have tried to borrow, sometimes revising in the process, those productive aspects of dialogue that compositionists already are using and explore those additional avenues that seemed to be lacking in composition's understanding of dialogism. The understanding of dialogic pedagogy I have posited is multilayered, and I have attempted to elaborate the various ways that I understand dialogue to function productively in the processes of creating discourse and in learning how to create it, processes that I see as overlapping and complementary. The various types of dialogue—internal, students/text, student/student, teacher/ student, and student/"public" audience—all are necessary for the development of students as competent writers who can produce written documents capable of carrying on the work of a literate society.

In short, a comprehensive dialogic pedagogy would recognize that knowledge unfolds in the process of attempting to communicate with others, what Kent calls communicative communicate with others, what Kent calls communicative interaction; in the give–and–take of this process, people come to know themselves, other people, and something about the concrete world. Another important component would be the development of students' ability to engage in dialogue with internalized others—what is traditionally called reflective thought. However, the goal of internal dialogue is "ideological becoming," a relational rather than personal concept of knowing—that is, the recognition of how one's personal knowledge is related to the knowledge of various communities and the unequal power structures that affect that interaction. Growing out of internal dialogue is students' dialogic engagement with written texts that already exist. In addition, as students encounter the voices of others in written documents, these voices help shape their internally persuasive discourse.

Peer criticism, another component of dialogic pedagogy, is one of the most productive ways that students in a writing class engage in communicative interaction because they are dealing with concrete audiences whose responses are timely enough to be considered, incorporated or not, responded to or not, while the students are composing. Dialogic pedagogy would also encourage students to address written documents to "public" audiences with the purpose of making a difference or having some effect on those they address, because the closer composition pedagogy comes to mirroring the actual rhetorical situations of public discourse the more effective the pedagogy is likely to be.

What has been missing in traditional concepts of dialogic pedagogy is an acknowledgment of differences among students and how the unequal social structures of society at large—structures related to racism, sexism, and classism—affect classroom settings in ways that disadvantage some and privilege others. I have tried to address this issue by exploring Code's revision of traditional epistemology and Welch's concept of communicative ethics as ways to help instructors and students become conscious of the ways democratic dialogue can be curtailed by uneven access to dialogic interaction and to assist them in discovering ways that avoid reproducing the negative effect of sexism, racism, and classism in composition class-rooms. Most importantly, a comprehensive dialogic pedagogy is one of inclusion; it is a pedagogy that acts to encourage all students to attempt to find a place in higher education regard-less of their particular "differences."

As dialogism becomes more and more central to composi-tion theory and pedagogy, it is essential that compositionists strive to break out of narrow ideological orientations and to embrace a more comprehensive notion of dialogism. The synthetic, functional dialogism that I have sketched here is but a beginning. What is needed now is more full-scale investiga-tions into the social and psychological dynamics of dialogic interaction. Such investigations could eventually contribute to an even fuller and more useful dialogism appropriate for the composition classroom. What *is* certain, though, is that dialogism is fundamental to modern composition pedagogy. Only through dialogue will students learn to be able to adopt a subject position in the conversation of humankind.

Notes

1. In fact, without the emphasis on an autonomous, solitary self-expressive writer, expressivism largely collapses into a social theory of writing. Moreover, doing so alleviates the theoretical tension caused by the conflict between

concepts of an autonomous, solitary author and that author's need for immediate feedback from others.

2. I am grateful to Professor Gary A. Olson for this method of using journals in composition classes.

Works Cited and Consulted

Abercrombie, M.L.J. *The Anatomy of Judgment*. London: Hutchinson, 1960.

Arnett, Ronald C. *Dialogic Education: Conversation About Ideas and Between Persons*. Carbondale: Southern Illinois UP, 1992.

—. "Toward Phenomenological Dialogue." *Western Journal of Speech Communication* 45 (1981): 201-12.

Aronowitz, Stanley. "Mass Culture and the Eclipse of Reason: The Implications for Pedagogy." *College English* 38 (1977): 768-74.

Ashton-Jones, Evelyn. "Feminist Critique of Collaborative Learning." Unpublished manuscript, 1992.

Bakhtin, M.M. *Art and Answerability: Early Philosophical Essays by M.M. Bakhtin*. Ed. Michael Holquist and Vadim Liapunov. Trans. Vadim Liapunov. Austin: U of Texas P, 1990.

—. *The Dialogic Imagination: Four Essays*. Trans. Caryl Emerson. Ed. Michael Holquist. Austin: U of Texas P, 1981.

—. *Problems of Dostoevsky's Poetics.* Ed. and Trans. Caryl
   Emerson. Theory and History of Literature 8.
   Minneapolis: U of Minnesota P, 1984.

—. *Speech Genres and Other Late Essays.* Ed. Caryl Emerson
   and Michael Holquist. Trans. Vern W. McGee.
   Austin: U of Texas P, 1986.

Bakhtin, Mikhail/V. N. Volosinov. *Marxism and the
   Philosophy of Language.* 1929. Trans. Ladislav Matejka
   and I.R. Titunik. Cambridge: Harvard UP, 1986.

Bator, Paul. "Aristotelian and Rogerian Rhetoric." *College
   Composition and Communication* 31 (1980): 427-32.

Bauer, Dale M. *Feminist Dialogics: A Theroy of Failed
   Community.* Albany: State U of New York P, 1988.

Baumlin, James S. "Persuasion, Rogerian Rhetoric, and
   Imaginative Play." *Rhetoric Society Quarterly* 7 (1987):
   33-44.

Bazerman, Charles. *The Informed Writer: Uning Sources in
   the Disciplines.* 3rd ed. Boston: Houghton, 1989.

—. "A Relationship between Writing and Reading: The
   Conversational Model." *College English* 41 (1980): 656-
   61.

—. *Shaping Written Knowledge: The Genre and Activity of the
   Experimental Article in Science.* Madison: U of
   Wisconsin P, 1988.

Beade, Pedro. "More Comments on 'Social Construction, Language, and the Authority of Knowledge: A Bibliographic Essay.'" *College English* 49 (1987): 707-08.

Berlin, James A. "Contemporary Composition: The Major Pedagogical Theories." *College English* 44 (1982): 765-77.

—. "Rhetoric and Ideology in the Writing Class." *College English* 50 (1988): 447-94.

—. *Rhetoric and Reality: Writing Instruction in American Colleges, 1900-1985.* Urbana, IL: NCTE, 1987.

Bialostosky, Don H. "Liberal Education, Writing, and the Dialogic Self." *Contending with Words: Composition and Rhetoric in a Postmodern Age.* Ed. Patricia Harkin and John Schilb. New York: MLA, 1991. 11-22.

Bizzell, Patricia. "Rev. of *Invention as a Social Act,* by Karen Burke LeFevre." *College Composition and Communication* 38 (1987): 485-86.

Bleich, David. *The Double Perspective: Language, Literacy and Social Relations.* New York: Oxford UP, 1988.

Brandt, Deborah. *Literacy as Involvement: The Acts of Writers, Readers, and Texts.* Carbondale: Southern Illinois UP, 1990.

—. "Review: Versions of Literacy." *College English* 47 (1985): 128-38.

—. "Social Foundations of Reading and Writing." *Reader* 12 (1984): 14-21.

—. "Toward an Understanding of Context in Composition." *Written Communication* 3 (1986): 139-57.

Brent, Doug. "Young, Becker and Pike's 'Rogerian' Rhetoric: A Twenty-Year Reassessment." *College English* 53 (1991): 452-66.

Bruffee, Kenneth A. "Collaborative Learning and the 'Conversation of Mankind.'" *College English* 46 (1984): 635-52.

—. *Short Course in Writing.* 3rd ed. Boston: Little, 1985.

—. *Short Course in Writing.* 4th ed. HarperCollins, 1993.

—. "Social Construction, Language, and the Authority of Knowledge: A Bibliographic Essay." *College English* 48 (1986): 773-90.

Burke, Kenneth. *A Grammar of Motives.* 1945. Berkeley: U of California P, 1969.

—. *The Philosophy of Literary Form: Studies in Symbolic Action.* 3rd ed. Berkeley: U of California P, 1973.

Carter, Michael. "What is *Advanced* about Advanced Composition?: A Theory of Expertise in Writing." *Teaching Advanced Composition: Why and How.* Ed.

Katherine H. Adams and John L. Adams. Portsmouth, NH: Boynton, 1991. 59-70.

Clark, Gregory. *Dialogue, Dialectic, and Conversation: A Social Perspective on the Function of Writing.* Carbondale: Southern Illinois UP, 1990.

Clark, Katerina, and Michael Holquist. *Mikhail Bakhtin.* Cambridge: Harvard UP, 1984.

Code, Lorraine. *What Can She Know? Feminist Theory and the Construction of Knowledge.* Ithaca, NY: Cornell UP, 1991.

Coe, Richard M. "Closed System Composition." *ETC: A Review of General Semantics* 32.4 (1975): 403-12.

Comprone, Joseph J. "The Function of Text in a Dialogic Writing Course." Kentucky Philological Association. Louisville, Mar. 1987. ERIC ED 284 239.

Cooper, Marilyn M. "The Ecology of Writing." *Writing As Social Action.* Ed. Marilyn M. Cooper and Michael Holzman. Portsmouth, NH: Boynton, 1989. 1-13.

Covino, William A. *The Art of Wondering: A Revisionist Return to the History of Rhetoric.* Portsmouth, NH: Boynton, 1988.

—. "Defining Advanced Composition: Contributions from the History of Rhetoric." *Journal of Advanced Composition* 8 (1988): 113-22.

—. *Forms of Wondering: A Dialogue on Writing for Writers.* Portsmouth, NH: Boynton, 1990.

—. "Grammar of Advanced Writing." *Teaching Advanced Composition: Why and How.* Ed. Katherine H. Adams and John L. Adams. Portsmouth, NH: Boynton, 1991. 31-42.

Crowley, Sharon. *A Teacher's Introduction to Deconstruction.* Urbana, IL: NCTE, 1989.

Crusius, Timothy. "Kenneth Burke's *Auscultation*: A "Destruction" of Marxist Dialectic and Rhetoric." *Rhetorica* 6 (1988): 355-79.

Davidson, Donald. *Inquires into Truth and Interpretation.* Oxford, England: Clarendon P, 1984.

Ede, Lisa. "Is Rogerian Rhetoric Really Rogerian?" *Rhetoric Review* 3 (1984): 40-47.

Elbow, Peter. "Closing My Eyes as I Speak: An Argrment for Ignoring Audience." *College English* 49 (1987): 50-69.

—. *Sharing and Responding.* New York: Random, 1989.

—. *Writing Without Teachers.* London: Oxford UP. 1973.

—. *Writing With Power: Techniques for Mastering the Writing Process.* New York: Oxford UP, 1981.

Elbow, Peter, and Pat Belanoff. *A Community of Writers: A Workshop Course in Writing.* New York: Random, 1989.

Emerson, Caryl. "The Outer Word and Inner Speech: Bahktin, Vygotsky, and the Internalization of Language." *Critical Inquiry* 10 (1983): 245-64.

Ewald, Helen Rothschild. "The Implied Reader in Persuasive Discourse." *Journal of Advanced Composition* 8 (1988): 167-78.

Faigley, Lester. "Competing Theories of Process: A Critique and a Proposal." *College English* 48 (1986): 527-42.

Fiore, Kyle, and Nan Elsasser. "'Strangers No More': A Liberatory Literacy Curriculum." *College English* 44 (1982): 115-28. Rpt. in *Freire for the Classroom: A Sourcebook for Liberatory Teaching.* Ed. Ira Shor. Portsmouth, NH: Boynton, 1987. 87-103.

Fish, Stanley. *Self-Consuming Artifacts: The Experience of Seventeenth-Century Literature.* Berkeley: U of California P, 1972.

Fox, Thomas J. *The Social Uses of Writing: Politics and Pedagogy.* Norwood, NY: Ablex, 1990.

Freire, Paulo. *Cultural Action for Freedom.* Cambridge: *Harvard Educational Review* and Center for the Study of Development and Social Change, 1970.

—. *Education for Critical Consciousness.* New York: Seabury, 1973.

—. Interview. "History, *Praxis*, and Change: Paulo Freire and the Politics of Literacy." By Gary A. Olson. *(Inter)views: Cross-Disciplinary Perspective on Rhetoric and Literacy.* Ed. Gary A. Olson and Irene Gale. Carbondale: Southern Illinois UP, 1991. 155-68.

—. *Pedagogy of the Oppressed.* New York: Seabury, 1970.

—. *Politics of Education: Culture, Power, and Liberation.* South Hadley, MA: Bergin, 1985.

Gere, Anne Ruggles. *Writing Groups: History, Theory, and Implications.* Carbondale: Southern Illinois UP, 1987.

Gergen, Kenneth A. "The Social Constructionist Movement in Modern Psychology." *American Psychologist* 40 (1985): 266-75.

Giroux, Henry A. *Ideology, Culture, and the Process of Schooling.* Philadelphia: Temple UP, 1981.

—. "Introduction." *The Politics of Education: Culture, Power, and Liberation.* By Paulo Freire. South Hadley, MA: Bergin, 1985. xi-xxv.

—. "Literacy and the Pedagogy of Voice and Political Empowerment." *Educational Theory* 38 (1988): 61-75.

—. "Paulo Freire and the Politics of Postcolonialism." *Journal of Advanced Composition* 12 (1992): 15-26.

—. *Schooling and the Struggle for Public Life: Critical Pedagogy in the Modern Age.* Minneapolis: U of Minnesota P, 1988.

—. "Theories of Reproduction and Resistance in the New Sociology of Education: A Critical Analysis." *Harvard Educational Review* 53 (1983): 257-93.

—. *Theory and Resistance in Education: A Pedagogy for the Opposition.* South Hadley, MA: Bergin, 1983.

Greene, Stuart. "Toward a Dialectical Theory of Composing." *Rhetoric Review* 9 (1990): 149-72.

Gumperz, John J. "Interactional Sociolinguistics in the Study of Sociology." *The Social Construction of Literacy.* Ed. Jenny Cook-Gumperz. Cambridge: Cambridge UP, 1986.

Hairston, Maxine. "Carl Roger's Alternative to Traditional Rhetoric." *College Composition and Communication* 27 (1977): 373-77.

—. *Contemporary Rhetoric.* 3rd. ed. Boston: Houghton, 1982.

—. "Using Carl Roger's Communication Theories in the Classroom." *Rhetoric Review* 1 (1982): 50-55.

Harris, Jeanette. *Expressive Discourse.* Dallas: Southern Methodist UP, 1990.

Hart, Roderick P., and Don M. Burks. "Rhetorical Sensitivity and Social Interaction." *Speech Monographs* 39 (1971): 75-91.

Hartwell, Patrick. "Grammar, Grammars, and the Teaching of Grammar." *College English* 47 (1985): 105-27.

Holquist, Michael. *Dialogism: Bakhtin and His World.* London: Routledge, 1990.

Hymes, Dell. "Models of the Interactions of Language and Social Life." *Directions in Sociolinguistics.* Ed. Dell Hymes and John J. Gumperz. New York: Holt, 1972.

James, Charity. *Young Lives at Stake: A Reappraisal of Secondary Schools.* London: Collins, 1968.

Jarratt, Susan C. "Feminism and Composition: The Case for Conflict." *Contending with Words: Composition and Rhetoric in a Postmodern Age.* Ed. Patricia Harkin and John Schilb. New York: MLA, 1991. 105-23.

Johannesen, Richard L. "The Emerging Concept of Communication as Dialogue." *Quarterly Journal of Speech* 57 (1971): 373-82.

Johnson, Thomas S. "A Comment on 'Collaborative Learning and the Conversation of Mankind.'" *College English* 48 (1986): 76.

Jones, Steven Jeffrey. "The Logic of Question and Answer and the Hermeneutics of Writing." *Journal of Advanced Composition* 8 (1988): 12-21.

Karis, Bill. "Conflict in Collaboration: A Burkean Perspective." *Rhetoric Review* 8 (1989): 113-26.

Kent, Thomas. "Beyond System: The Rhetoric of Paralogy." *College English* 51 (1989): 492-507.

—. "Externalism and the Production of Discourse." *Journal of Advanced Composition* 12 (1992): 57-74.

—. "On the Very Idea of a Discourse Community." *College Composition and Communication* 42 (1991): 425-45.

—. "Paralogic Hermeneutics and the Possibilities of Rhetoric." *Rhetoric Review* 8 (1989): 24-42.

Kinneavy, James L. "The Relation of the Whole to the Part in Interpretation Theory and in the Composition Process." *The Territory of Language: Linguistics, Stylistics, and the Teaching of Composition*. Ed. Donald A. McQuade. Carbondale: Southern Illinois UP, 1986. 292-312.

Klancher, John. "Bakhtin's Rhetoric." *Reclaiming Pedagogy*. Ed. Patricia Donahue and Ellen Quandrahl. Carbondale: Southern Illinois UP, 1989.

Knoblauch, C.H. "Critical Teaching and Dominant Culture." *Resistance and Composition*." Ed. C. Mark Hurlbert and Michael Blitz. Portsmouth, NH: Boynton, 1991. 12-21.

—. "Rhetorical Constructions: Dialogue and Commitment." *College English* 50 (1988): 125-40.

Kuhn, Thomas S. *The Structure of Scientific Revolutions.* 2nd ed. Chicago: U of Chicago P, 1970.

Lassner, Phyllis. "Feminist Responses to Rogerian Argument." *Rhetoric Review* 8 (1990): 220-31.

LeFevre, Karen Burke. *Invention as a Social Action.* Carbondale: Southern Illinois UP, 1987.

Lindemann, Erika. "Ken Macrorie: A Review Essay." *College English* 44 (1982): 358-67.

Lunsford, Andrea. "Aristotelian vs. Rogerian Argument: A Reassessment." *College Composition and Communication* 30 (1979): 146-51.

—. " Nature of Composition Studies." *Introduction to Composition Studies.* Ed. Erika Lindemann and Gary Tate. New York: Oxford UP, 1991. 3-14.

Macrorie, Ken. *Telling Writing.* 4th ed. Portsmouth, NH: Boynton, 1985.

—. *Uptaught.* New York: Hayden, 1970.

Maimon, Elaine. "Talking to Strangers." *College Composition and Communication* 30 (1979): 364-69.

Mason, Edwin. *Collaborative Learning.* New York: Agathon, 1972.

McClish, Glen. "Some Less-Acknowledged Links: Rhetorical Theory, Interpersonal Communication, and the Tradition of the Liberal Arts." *Rhetoric Society Quarterly* 20 (1990): 105-18.

Miller, Susan. *Rescuing the Subject: A Critical Introduction to Rhetoric and the Writer.* Carbondale: Southern Illinois UP, 1989.

Murray, Donald M. "The Explorers of Inner Space." *Learning by Teaching: Selected Articles on Writing and Teaching.* Upper Montclair, NJ: Boynton, 1982. 3-7.

—. "The Interior View: One Writer's Philosophy of Composition." *Learning by Teaching: Selected Articles on Writing and Teaching.* Upper Montclair, NJ: Boynton, 1982. 7-14.

—. "Teaching the Other Self: The Writer's First Reader." *Learning by Teaching: Selected Articles on Writing and Teaching.* Upper Montclair, NJ: Boynton, 1982. 164-72.

—. "What Makes Students Write." *Expecting the Unexpected: Teaching Myself—and Others–to Read and Write.* Portsmouth, NH: Boynton, 1989. 108-12.

Myers, Greg. "Reality, Consensus, and Reform in the Rhetoric of Composition Teaching." *College English* 48 (1986): 154-74.

Neel, Jasper. *Plato, Derrida, and Writing.* Carbondale: Southern Illinois UP, 1988.

Oakeshott, Michael. "The Voice of Poetry and the 'Conversations of Mankind.'" *Rationalism in Politics.* New York: Basic, 1962. 196-247.

Ong, Walter J. *Ramus, Method, and the Decay of Dialogue.* Cambridge: Harvard UP, 1958.

—. "The Writer's Audience Is Always a Fiction." *PMLA* 90 (1975): 9-21.

Perelman, Chaim. "The Dialectical Method and the Part Played by the Interlocutor in Dialogue." *The Idea of Justice and the Problem of Argument.* Trans. John Petrie. New York: Humanities P, 1963. 161-67.

—. *The Realm of Rhetoric.* Trans. William Kluback. Notre Dame: U of Notre Dame P, 1969.

Perelman, Chaim, and L. Olbrechts-Tyteca. *The New Rhetoric.* Notre Dame: U of Notre Dame P, 1969.

Rasinsky, Timothy V., and Sally Natenson-Mejia. "Commentary: Learning to Read, Learning Community Considerations of the Social Contexts for Literacy Instruction." *Reading Teacher* 41 (1987): 260-65.

Reither, James A. "Writing and Knowing: Toward Redefining the Writing Process." *College English* 47 (1985): 620-28.

Rogers, Carl R. *Client-Centered Therapy.* Boston: Houghton, 1951.

—. *On Becoming a Person.* Boston: Houghton, 1961.

Rohman, D. Gordon, and Albert O. Wlecke. *Pre-Writing: The Construction and Application of Models for Concept Formation in Writing.* U.S. Office of Education Cooperative Research Project No. 2174. East Lansing: Michigan State U, 1964.

Rorty, Richard. *Philosophy and the Mirror of Nature.* Princeton, NJ: Princeton UP, 1980.

Sanchez, Raul, "Beyond Process: Pedagogical Implications of Post-Process Theory." Unpublished Manuscript, 1992.

Schilb, John. "Rev. of *Freire for the Classroom.*" Ed. Ira Shor. *Journal of Advanced Composition* 9 (1989): 191-94.

Schuster, Charles I. "Mikhail Bakhtin as Rhetorical Theorist." *College English* 47 (1985): 594-607.

Shor, Ira. *Critical Teaching and Everyday Life.* Chicago: U of Chicago P, 1987.

—. ed. *Freire for the Classroom: A Sourcebook for Liberatory Teaching.* Portsmouth, NH: Boynton, 1987.

Shor, Ira, and Paulo Freire. *A Pedagogy for Liberation.* South Hadley, MA: Bergin, 1987.

Smit, David. "Some Difficulties with Collaborative Learning." *Journal of Advanced Composition* 9 (1989): 45-58.

Stewart, Donald C. *The Authentic Voice: A Pre-Writing Approach to Student Writing.* Dubuque, IA: Brown, 1972.

—. "Collaborative Learning and Composition: Boon or Bane?" *Rhetoric Review* 7 (1988): 58-83.

Stewart, John. "Foundations of Dialogic Communication." *Quarterly Journal of Speech* 64 (1978): 183-201.

Stygall, Gail. "Teaching Freire in North America: A Review Essay of Ira's Shor's *Freire for the Classroom: A Sourcebook for Liberatory Teaching.*" *Journal of Teaching Writing* 8 (1989): 113-25.

Teich, Nathaniel. "Rogerian Problem-Solving and the Rhetoric of Argumentation." *Journal of Advanced Composition* 7 (1987): 52-61.

Ulmer, Gregory. *Applied Grammatology: Post(e)-Pedagogy from Jacques Derrida to Joseph Beuys.* Baltimore: Johns Hopkins UP, 1985.

—. *Telethory: Grammatology in the Age of Video.* New York: Routledge, 1989.

Villanueva, Victor, Jr. "Considerations for American Freirestas." *The Politics of Writing Instruction: Postsecondary.* Ed. Richard Bullock and John Trimbur. Portsmouth, NH: Boynton, 1991. 247-62.

Vygotsky, Lev. *Thought and Language*. Cambridge: MIT P, 1962.

Welch, Sharon. "An Ethic of Solidarity and Difference." *Postmodernism, Feminism, and Cultural Politics: Redrawing Educational Boundaries*. Ed. Henry A. Giroux. Albany: State U of New York P, 1991. 83-99.

Young, Richard E., Alton E. Becker, and Kenneth L. Pike. *Rhetoric: Discovery and Change*. New York: Harcourt, 1970.

Zappan, James P. "Carl P. Rogers and Political Rhetoric." *Pre/Text* 1 (1980): 95-113.

Zeiger, William. "A Dialectical Model for College Composition." *Freshman English News* 16 (1987): 14-16.

Index